D1257828

A
BATTLEFIELD
ATLAS

OF THE
AMERICAN
REVOLUTION

by Craig L. Symonds
Cartography by William J. Clipson

The Nautical & Aviation Publishing Company of America, Inc.

Copyright © 1986 by
The Nautical & Aviation Publishing Company of America, Inc.
101 W. Read Street
Suite 314
Baltimore, MD. 21201

All rights reserved.
No part of this book may be reproduced
in any manner without written permission from the
publisher, except in the case of brief quotations
embodied in critical articles and reviews.

Library of Congress Catalog Number: 86-063201

ISBN: 0-933852-53-3

Printed in the United States of America.
Second printing, March 1987
Third printing, March 1988
Fourth printing, February 1991

FOR MY
MOTHER AND FATHER

Contents

KEY TO MAP SYMBOLS

▬	Infantry Units
▨	Former position of infantry units
⬍	Infantry
⬍	Cavalry or mounted dragoons
■ ■ ■ ■ ■	Dispersed infantry units
● ● ● ● ●	Skirmish line
⟹	Intended line of advance
- - - ➤	Actual line of advance
▤ ▩	Army headquarters
⫽ ⫽ ⫽	Artillery (depicts location, not precise number of guns)
⛴	Sea-going warships
⊥	Gunboats
✕ ▢ ▫	Forts
⎍⎍⎍⎍⎍	Field fortifications
⸙⸙⸙⸙⸙⸙	Bridge of boats
x—x—x—x—x	Fence
o—o—o—o—o	Log-and-chain boom (river barrier)
✬	Site of battle or skirmish

Introduction

The bloodshed at Lexington and Concord on April 19, 1775 launched a fratricidal war that lasted eight years. At its end a new nation emerged, and England, arguably the most powerful nation in the world at the time, was brought low not only by the loss of the richest jewel in its Empire, but because the war provided an opportunity for France, England's arch-enemy, to gain revenge for its recent defeat in the Seven Years War. In addition, the American Revolution was a very human war, fought with weapons that brought the opposing forces to close quarters with one another, and, for the most part, between forces that spoke the same language. The standard infantry weapon of both armies was the flintlock musket. It was a smooth bore (not rifled) weapon about five feet long that could be fitted with a bayonet that turned it into a six foot pike. The smoothbore muskets were generally inaccurate beyond about eighty yards. Since it took at least eight separate steps to load, prime, and fire the weapon, the standard infantry tactic of eighteenth century armies was to march in a tight formation to within about 50-60 yards of the enemy, fire one volley, and then charge with the bayonet. It took iron discipline to execute this maneuver, and even greater discipline to receive it without flinching. For that reason, veteran troops were generally far more reliable in battle than militia or raw recruits. Yet in the end it was the rebellious rabble and not the disciplined veterans that emerged triumphant.

This slim volume is intended to provide a visual and narrative overview of the principal military engagements of the war of the American Revolution. As in our companion volume, *A Battlefield Atlas of the Civil War,* the object here is clarity more than detail. Rather than produce a cartographic portrayal that included the movement of every unit, we sought to produce maps where the important strategic and tactical maneuvers could be perceived at a glance. All the maps have a north-south axis, but are drawn to different scales, and for that reason a bar scale is included on each map.

It is important to be aware that the boxes used to indicate the location of armed units are not intended to show the precise number of regiments or brigades involved in each action. Instead, the number of boxes indicates the *proportional* strength of the two sides. Indeed, showing the actual number of regiments or brigades involved would be confusing rather than clarifying because the strength of individual units varied so greatly not only between the two armies, but within each army. Officially American Continental Army regiments were composed of eight companies of 76 men each. Including officers, each regiment had a paper strength of just over 700. In practice, however, that number varied dramatically. Some regiments had a total strength of less than 100, and often brigades (supposedly composed of several regiments) totalled only 200-300. Eventually unit designations in the American army derived as much from the rank of the commander as from the number of men in the unit. If a Brigadier General commanded, it was, *ipso facto,* a brigade though it might have only 350 men, as did Brigadier General Hugh Mercer's brigade at the Battle of Princeton (Map # 11).

British regiments varied in size from about 300 to over 1,000, though regiments of 1,000 were rare. Each regiment was supposed to consist of ten companies of 38 men each plus a captain, two lieutenants, and a handful of non-commissioned officers. Two of the ten companies were designated as elite units. One, made up of the tallest and strongest men, was called the grenadier company even though the men no longer carried or threw grenades. Another was composed of the most physically fit troops, chosen for their speed and agility and was designated the light infantry company. The grenadiers were the shock troops of the British army and the light infantry was generally used as an advance guard or to pursue a defeated enemy. It was common to detach these elite companies from their regular regiments for special missions such as the march to Concord to seize rebel arms in April of 1775. Cavalry played a relatively small role in the war; only in the southern campaigns of 1780-81 did cavalry help determine the outcome of a battle. Dragoons were essentially mounted infantry, though they also often fought from horseback.

Although, virtually all of the maps in this book are original, they have been compiled from a number of sources. The British produced the best contemporary battlefield maps for they were professional soldiers fighting in unfamiliar terrain. Don Higginbotham's *Atlas of the American Revolution* (1974) contains 49 contemporary maps, most of which were produced by British cartographers in the 1780s. The Americans produced few useful maps at all. Especially in irregular warfare, American commanders might issue orders with reference to known local landmarks that have since disappeared. If necessary, they might sketch out the rough features of a battlefield, but seldom in the kind of detail that is useful two hundred years later. Of course maps of the battlefields have been drawn subsequently by historians and cartographers, many of them employed by the National Parks Service, and we are in debt to several generations of artists who have surveyed the ground and produced useful maps of the more important battlefields. In many cases, the degree of forestation, the area under cultivation, and even the location of swamps and streams have changed in the two centuries since the war. In the production of these maps, therefore, the detail has been drawn whenever possible from contemporary sources, including narrative descriptions, in order to represent the nature of the terrain at the time of the battle.

The text accompanying each of the maps is necessarily brief, but I have made an effort to go beyond the mere description of troop movements to include a discussion of the personalities and motivations of the principal commanders on both sides. When appropriate, I have used the words of the participants themselves. In every case the interpretations offered are my own.

I am particularly grateful to Bill Clipson whose perfectionism in rendering has made these maps so clear. For any error that might exist on any map, I am solely responsible. In addition I want to thank Major Don Alexander of the United States Army, Professor James C. Bradford of Texas A & M University, and Professor John Huston of the Naval Academy each of whom read the manuscript and made many helpful comments.

Craig L. Symonds
Annapolis, Maryland

Prologue:
Boston Harbor

In 1763 the city of Boston was the foremost Atlantic seaport in the English colonies and the political and cultural center of New England. In the preceeding half decade the citizens of Boston had celebrated many victories. First there had been the English conquest of the French fortress of Louisburg at the entrance to the St. Lawrence River in 1758, an expedition in which a large number of Massachusetts sons had participated. Then a year later came news of General Wolfe's victory over Montcalm and the capture of Quebec, though the public joy was muted somewhat by the information that the young and handsome Wolfe had lost his life in the victory. The next year a new king, George III, had come to the throne to preside over the victory in the Seven Years War with France in 1763. For the citizens of Boston, the news of the Peace of Paris meant not having to worry about French invasions from the north or French encouragement of Indian raids against the western settlements.

But there was soon to be some disquieting news in Boston. Parliament in 1764 passed a Revenue Act that levied a tax on imported molasses, from which sugar was made. This bill revived an old act which had obligated the colonials to pay a duty of 6 pence a barrel on molasses, but which virtually everyone had ignored. The new Revenue Act halved that duty, but at the same time made it clear that revenue inspectors would enforce collection. The Boston merchants grumbled, partly because it would affect their purse, but partly too because they saw it as a straw in the wind. While Americans generally conceded to Parliament the right to regulate trade within the Empire, most

Americans disguised as Indians dump tea into Boston Harbor from the deck of an East Indiaman on the night of December 16, 1773. This act provoked harsh repressive measures by the ministry of Lord North and marked a crucial turning point in the relations between Britain and the American colonies. From a 19th century lithograph. (NA)

also believed that bills for the express purpose of raising revenue had to originate in the assemblies of those who would pay the tax.

Two years later Parliament passed another revenue bill: this one required the colonials to affix an official stamp, like a notary's seal, on all wills, titles, and other legal documents, as well as on playing cards, dice, and almanacs. The purpose of the bill was clear: not to regulate trade, but to raise revenue. The money was needed, British authorities explained, to help defray the cost of the recent war with France and the continued expense of defending the colonies. The outbreak of opposition to this Stamp Act was immediate and widespread. If the Empire needed revenue, some colonists argued, colonial assemblies might offer funds as a free gift, but they should not be forced to contribute by the decision of a legislative body over three thousand miles away. Moreover, against what enemy did the colonies require defense? The war was over and the French evicted from Canada. Despite Pontiac's rebellion near Fort Detroit, the American colonists no longer believed that the protection of the British Army was essential to their own survival.

The British were stunned by the American reaction to the Stamp Act. In England subjects paid a stamp tax with no complaint, and at much higher rates than those being asked of the American colonists. And after all, the great bulk of the national debt, which had doubled during the war with France, had been incurred in the defense of those very colonies. Wasn't it only reasonable that the colonials assume at least some of the burden of the expense? Still, the outcry in the American colonies was so sharp and so universal that after passing a Declaratory Act which asserted the right of Parliament to enact legislation for the colonies "in all cases whatsoever," the new Rockingham ministry repealed the hated Stamp Act. The next year (1767) Americans were delighted to learn that their friend William Pitt had once again been named Prime Minister, but they were distressed to learn that his Chancellor of the Exchequer, Charles Townshend, had persuaded Parliament to pass a series of new revenue bills that levied duties on lead, paper, paint, glass, and tea. Americans did not see the Townshend Acts as an effort to regulate trade, but recognized them for what they were: another effort to raise money. In their view, the distinction was not so much internal versus external taxes, but bills for *taxation* as opposed to bills for *regulation*. In that sense, the very purpose of the Townshend Acts made them unconstitutional. Colonial assemblies protested against these new duties nearly as much as they had the Stamp Act, and several, including Massachusetts, determined to boycott the goods so taxed.

In 1768 the British sent the first troops to Boston that were meant not to protect the colonists from the French, but to enforce the new laws. A year and a half later, on March 5, 1770 the perhaps inevitable clash between these soldiers and colonial civilians took place in front of the Boston customhouse when a group of ten British soldiers, after being pelted by stones, fired on a mob, killing five and wounding seven others. Bostonians became so outraged by this "massacre" that the troops had to be removed to Castle William in the harbor in part, at least, for their own safety.

Ironically, two months earlier a new ministry under Lord North had repealed the Townshend duties. The British discovered that the Americans had begun to avoid the new duties by manufacturing their own lead, paint, paper, and glass. If that continued, such industries would undermine the usefulness of America as an outlet for British manufacturers. All of the duties, therefore, had been repealed—all, that is, except the tax on tea, a commodity which could not be grown in America.

Having won another political victory, most Americans were satisfied, and a confrontation on the tea tax might have been avoided altogether but for the passage of the Tea Act, which was not a tax bill at all, but an effort to revive the flagging finances of the East India Company. In 1773 the North ministry gave permission to the East India Company to ship its tea directly to the colonies, avoiding the expense (and the taxes) of the long trip to England. Because of the savings in transit, the tea could be sold in America well below the previous market price. Of course the colonials would have to pay the taxes on the tea, but even with the tax, the cost of the tea would be less than they previously had paid for untaxed tea from England. The East India Company got a market for its tea, the colonials got tea at a bargain rate, and the government gained some revenue to help retire the national debt. But this tea would be sold in America exclusively by agents specially commissioned to do so. The prospect of government-managed retailing was a precedent horrifying to American merchants. They refused to allow the tea to be unloaded in Boston Harbor. The vessels floated idly while delegations of Massachusetts "patriots" argued the issue with the Royal governor.

British Major General Thomas Gage was the man on the spot in the growing crisis in Boston. Unable to satisfy either the colonists or the North Ministry in London, he was replaced by William Howe in 1775. (NA)

On the night of December 16, 1773 the stalemate was broken when several score "Sons of Liberty," imperfectly disguised as Indians, marched down to the wharf, climbed aboard the ships, and proceeded to dump the tea overboard into the waters of Boston Harbor. Their act proved to be the last straw for a patient ministry. A series of prime ministers had attempted to accommodate American objections to "internal" taxes by withdrawing the hated Stamp Tax and all but eliminating the Townshend Acts as well, and still the colonists were not satisfied. The so-called "Boston Tea Party" ended British patience with American protests and led the North ministry to enact a series of punitive bills which the Americans quickly labeled the "Intolerable Acts."

The British troops who had been quartered in Fort William since the Boston "massacre" were shifted back to the city and the new Quartering Act (one of the Intolerables) required the city to shelter and feed them. Major General Thomas Gage arrived to assume command and was endowed simultaneously with civil authority as the new Royal Governor. Gage was no tyrant. He had spent much of his life in America fighting the French and he was more interested in finding a solution to the growing estrangement between colonies and crown than in dishing out punishment. Nevertheless, his orders were to enforce the Intolerable Acts and keep the port of Boston closed until its citizens paid 15,000 pounds for the destroyed tea.

The orders closing Boston Harbor went into effect at noon on June 1, 1774. The result was economic paralysis. The city might have starved but for the contributions of neighboring colonies that sent wheat, cattle, and sheep overland across the narrow Boston Neck. Far from isolating Boston, the British restrictions served to bind the colonies closer together. Gage formed a citizen's council, but most Bostonians refused to serve in Gage's Council. Instead they set up a "Provincial Congress" of their own in Concord and sent delegates to a "Continental Congress" which would meet in Philadelphia in September.

In Boston, meanwhile, Gage was becoming more and more concerned about the volatility of the situation. His men reported that citizens had taken powder and shot from the magazine on Quarry Hill in nearby Charlestown. Gage hoped to defuse the situation by preventing an arms build-up. On September 1, therefore, he dispatched 260 soldiers to Charlestown where they removed some 250 barrels of gunpowder: all that the colonials had left. Another detachment seized two cannons at Cambridge. Far from the calming effect Gage had hoped for, news of these forays brought several thousand armed and angry colonials to Boston. Rumors spread of British outrages: Boston bombarded, citizens killed, the city aflame. The excitement died down when these rumors proved to be false. Nevertheless, the experience showed what might happen if there were an armed confrontation. Gage was so concerned he began erecting fortifications across Boston Neck (see MAP# 3). At the same time, the local militia companies outside Boston began stockpiling arms.

As part of his continuing effort to disarm the colonials, Gage sent General Alexander Leslie to Salem in February 1775 to seize arms there. It was a charade. Leslie's men ran into a group of armed and apparently determined colonials. Given the circumstances, Leslie decided that discretion was appropriate. He looked around briefly, announced that he saw no arms, and returned to Boston.

Early in April, Gage received orders to be more assertive and energetic in his prosecution of the rebellious Americans. As a result, he decided to send a column into the countryside to seize a cache of stockpiled arms rumored to be at Concord. It was a short march; Concord was only sixteen miles away, just past the village of Lexington.

PART ONE

Early Campaigns

News of the bloodshed at Lexington and Concord (MAPS # 1-2) reached Philadelphia in five days. When the Second Continental Congress met there two weeks later on May 10, delegates knew that thousands of armed men had flocked to join the siege of the British garrison in Boston (see MAP # 3). Congress responded to the outbreak of violence by appointing a committee to investigate ways to secure additional military equipment. On June 14 the delegates voted to send rifle companies from the middle colonies and Virginia to join the forces outside Boston thereby creating, by implication at least, a Continental Army. The next day Congress appointed George Washington to command "all the continental forces, raised, or to be raised, for the defense of American liberty."

The selection of George Washington to command the rebel armies was politically clever and, as it turned out, even inspired. First of all he was from Virginia. That fact alone made him valuable for it established a tie between the southern colonies and the army in New England. John Hancock, President of the Congress and a man with military ambitions of his own, was the other logical candidate, but as a New Englander his appointment would not help tie the middle and southern colonies to the resistance in the same way Washington's would. It was Hancock's fellow New Englander, John Adams, who argued most eloquently and vehemently for Washington's selection. Second, Washington was a good choice because of his character. As a brash young man he had been unbecomingly ambitious and, as a land speculator, embarrassingly acquisitive. But in his middle age, he had developed the maturity, tolerance, and

A ragged line of "Minutemen" face British regulars on Lexington Green on April 19, 1775 in the battle that began the war. "If they want a war, let it begin here!" Captain John Parker is supposed to have told his seventy or so Minutemen. This drawing of the engagement is by Connecticut militiaman Amos Doolittle. (NA)

most of all, patience necessary to endure the repeated disappointments and frustrations of command in the early years of the war. Finally, and above all else, Washington was a man of impeccable personal standards. When Congress granted him broad discretionary powers in the darkest days of the war, he used them sparingly and judiciously. Dictatorship had no charms for him. He sought applause and praise to be sure, but he lacked the *hubris* to assume undelegated powers. Throughout the war he served at his own insistence without any pay (though he did keep a careful expense account), and he answered respectfully and subordinately the most fatuous of Congressional pronouncements.

Keeping the army intact was Washington's most serious and immediate problem. Throughout the early campaigns, the army continually threatened simply to melt away. Expiring enlistments often dictated the timing of a campaign: the American assault on Quebec (MAP # 6) as well as Washington's attacks at Trenton and Princeton (MAPS # 10-11) were prompted, at least in part, by that concern. Always distressed by this problem, Washington at times grew disgusted. At one point he addressed his troops with obvious anger: "The General is sorry to find that there are some soldiers so lost to all sense of honor and honesty as to leave the Army when there is the greatest necessity for their service: He calls upon the officers of every rank to exert themselves in putting a stop to it, and absolutely forbids any officer, under the rank of Brigadier General, discharging any officer or soldier or giving any permission to leave the camp on any pretense whatsoever."

Washington could not win the war with the troops available to him in 1775, but his job was to avoid losing it since the very existence of his army kept the rebellion alive. The independence of the United States, declared in the second summer of the war, rested entirely on the back of Washington's army. Cities and fortresses might fall, the Americans could lose battle after battle, but so long as Washington's army remained intact,

9

The selection of George Washington to command the Continental Army was perhaps the single most important decision of the Continental Congress. Patient, determined, and realistic, Washington held the American army together through the first crucial year of the war. Painting by Rembrandt Peale (NA).

Sir William Howe was a paradox: a skilled strategist and tactician, he outmaneuvered Washington at every opportunity, yet time after time he failed to apply the final stroke that might have crushed the rebel army.

the rebellion was alive. Washington's determination and persistence was the key to the survival of American hopes during the crucial early campaigns.

In addition to Washington, Congress also appointed four major generals and eight brigadiers. The selection of the four major generals was also politically motivated. Artemas Ward, the de facto commander of the troops outside Boston, received one appointment, Israel Putnam of Connecticut another. The other two were Charles Lee, a former officer in the British army, and Philip Schuyler, a veteran of the Seven Years War. Other than Washington, none of these men distinguished himself in the war.

Jealousy among officers was a serious problem in the American army. The earliest and perhaps clearest example was the feud between Benedict Arnold and Ethan Allen in upstate New York. Indeed, there was general distrust, if not open hostility, between officers from different states and sections, especially between men from New York and New England, and Washington and the Congress had to balance appointments carefully to avoid offending one group or another.

Another aspect of this same problem was the jealousy virtually all American officers felt of the foreign volunteers who came to America from Po-

land, Germany, or France. Often ambitious beyond their talents, these candidates for high rank presented their credentials to Congress and emerged as Brigadiers or Major Generals without so much as meeting an American soldier or facing a British musket. A few of these men proved to be assets to the American cause — notably the Pole Thaddeus Kosciuszko, the German Friedrich von Steuben, and the French Marquis de Lafayette — but others proved to be a detriment, and all had to face the suspicious resentment of American officers who had been in the field since the beginning and who looked upon these adventure-seekers as mere opportunists.

The troops were a mixed lot. Continental army regiments were the most reliable and state militia units were the least. The pay of a continental soldier was five dollars a month plus a clothing allowance. Occasionally Washington would offer a bounty, usually ten dollars, for reinlistment, but very few joined the American army to make money. In addition to the Continental troops, Washington frequently had to call upon local militia units. These were composed of troops of indifferent discipline who mustered for short periods to defend a particular community. They often refused to serve beyond a certain area or a specific time. Their fickleness agonized and frustrated Washington, and he remained suspicious of militia troops for the rest of his life. Though eleven of the states eventually designated dark blue as the official uniform color, the dominant uniform of all these troops was brown, with different color facings to indicate the state of origin. Many wore loose-fitting hunting shirts, generally fringed.

Washington's counterpart in the British Army was Sir William Howe, a man of manifest military talents whose family had a distinguished military heritage. An older brother, George, had been killed at Ticonderoga in the Seven Years War, and another brother, Richard, was an admiral. Howe was a court favorite and British hopes of salvaging the situation in American rested on him. Howe cherished hopes that the fratricidal war could be ended by compromise. His first experience in fighting the colonials was at Bunker Hill (see MAP # 4) and that nightmare marked him for life. That undisciplined farmers could inflict more than forty percent casualties on crack British regiments horrified him.

Howe's battlefield maneuvers were at times brilliant, and at other times lethargic. The New York campaign (see MAPS # 8-9) was an example of both his brilliance and his lethargy. He completely outmaneuvered the Americans on Long Island, did so again on Manhattan, and again during the campaign in Westchester County. But on each occasion he let Washington slip away when he might have crushed him utterly. Critics then and since have pondered this apparent schizophrenia. Some have assumed that Howe hesitated to apply the *coup de grace* because he was still hoping for a negotiated settlement; others insist that he had been intimidated by his experience at Bunker Hill; still others argue that Howe simply lacked the killer instinct. By the end of the first full year of war, the British had routed the Americans at every opportunity and thoroughly mauled Washington's rag tag army. But Howe failed to destroy the American army and Washington's counterattacks at Trenton and Princeton at the end of the year gave the rebels new life and new hope.

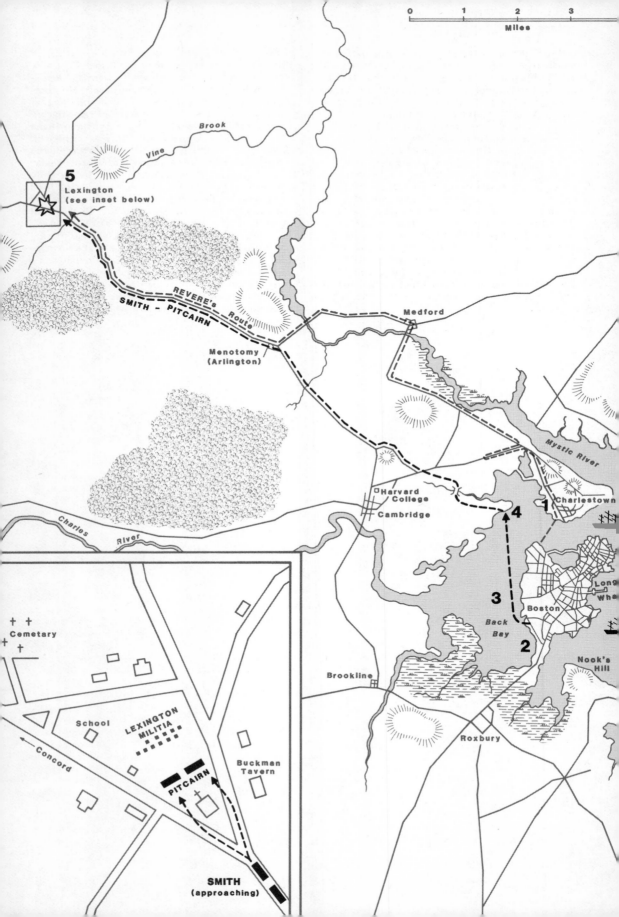

0 1 2 3
Miles

5
Lexington
(see inset below)

Brook

Vine

REVERE's Route

SMITH – PITCAIRN

Medford

Menotomy
(Arlington)

Mystic River

Charlestown

Harvard
College

Cambridge

4

1

Charles River

3

Back
Bay

Boston

Long
Wha

2

Nook's
Hill

Brookline

Roxbury

Cemetary

School

Concord

LEXINGTON
MILITIA

PITCAIRN

Buckman
Tavern

SMITH
(approaching)

MAP # 1

The Road to Lexington

April 19, 1775

For the expedition to Concord, Gage detached the light infantry and grenadiers from their regiments to form a separate command under Lieutenant Colonel Francis Smith. A Royal Marine, Major John Pitcairn, was to be second in command and lead the advance. It was common practice in eighteenth century armies to designate elite troops for an important mission, but Gage's decision separated the men from their known regimental officers and may have weakened command and control at a critical moment.

The expedition was supposed to move in secret, departing in the middle of the night and marching rapidly to avoid a confrontation with local militia units. But there were no secrets in Boston in 1775. Dr. Joseph Warren, an ardent "Patriot," learned of the plan almost immediately and on April 16 he dispatched Boston silversmith Paul Revere to warn John Hancock and Samuel Adams, members of the Continental Congress who were staying in nearby Lexington, of the British sortie. Revere returned that night and stopped in Charlestown (1) where he left word that when the British began to move, news of their route would be signalled from the steeple of North Church: one lantern if the British marched out over Boston Neck (2) through Roxbury and Brookline, and two if they took the short cut by boat across Back Bay (3).

At ten o'clock at night on April 18, the British sergeants shook their men awake for a night march. The men assembled in some confusion on Boston Common and boarded boats which took them across Back Bay to Lechmere Point (4) where they waded ashore. There they waited for some time for supplies to be distributed. While they lingered one or two may have noticed two lanterns winking from the steeple of North Church.

At the same time, Paul Revere was being rowed across Back Bay to Charlestown where he would begin his ride — the second in three days — to Lexington. Charged with the same mission as Revere, William Dawes took the land route over Boston Neck. As the British troops stepped out on the road toward Concord some sixteen miles away, they could hear the sound of bells and cannons in the distance alerting the countryside of their coming. As a precaution, Smith sent word back to Boston that he might need reinforcements before the day was over, but he kept his troops moving forward.

At four-thirty, in the first light of an early dawn, the British column came to Lexington (5), a small crossroads community of about 750 a little over halfway to Concord. At the outskirts of the town, Pitcairn heard a military drum beating assembly and he halted his advance column briefly and ordered the men to double their ranks and to load. Then he sent them forward at the double quick.

As the light infantry double-timed around both sides of the community church at the southern end of the common (see inset), they could see about seventy militiamen, drawn up in two ragged lines. They were not blocking the road to Concord, but their presence was a deliberate challenge and an implied threat. Many of them had been waiting since about one a.m. when Revere and Dawes had arrived with news of the British sortie. One hundred and forty "Minutemen" had answered the first call to arms, but that was three and a half hours before the arrival of the British, and only about half that number remained. Their commander was Captain John Parker, a 45-year-old veteran of the Indian Wars, and a former member of Rogers' Rangers.

As the leading troops of the British column rushed onto Lexington Green, Pitcairn rode to the front and called out to the militiamen to lay down their arms and disperse. Recognizing that his seventy odd militiamen had no chance to stand up to several hundred regulars, Parker passed the word to disperse, and men began to move slowly toward the edges of the common. But Pitcairn wanted them to lay down their arms as well. "Damn you!" he shouted. "Why don't you lay down your arms?" The British soldiers continued to rush onto the common, many of them shouting and cheering. Then someone fired a shot.

Each side insisted that the other had fired first. The question is academic now, but at the time it was critical, for the propaganda value was inestimable. In any case that first shot was followed by a full volley from one of the British platoons. Pitcairn called to his men to cease fire, but their blood was up and ignoring Pitcairn's frantic effort to restore order, the light infantrymen fired another volley and charged. The militiamen returned fire as they scurried for cover, but their aim was poor. In a matter of minutes, the British regulars had swept the militia from Lexington Green. One British soldier was lightly wounded while the militiamen suffered eight killed and ten wounded. By now Colonel Smith had arrived, and he and Pitcairn got their men under control, reformed them into columns, and allowed them the traditional victory volley before heading them up the road to Concord.

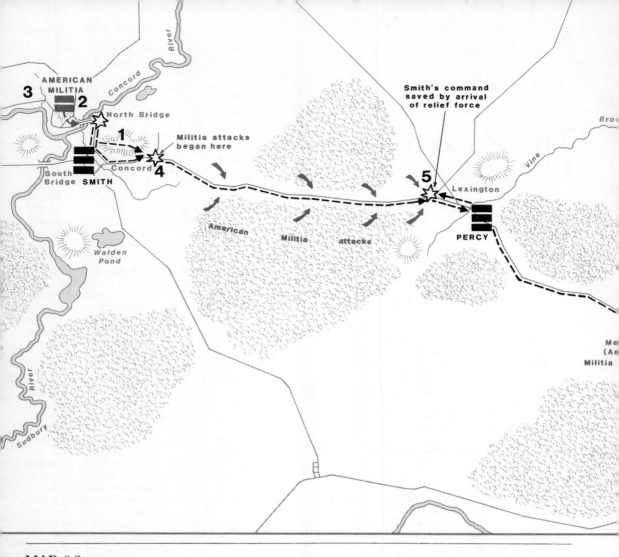

MAP # 2

Concord

April 19, 1775

News of the confrontation at Lexington raced ahead of the British column as it marched toward Concord. Neither Revere nor Dawes made it that far — both were intercepted by British patrols — but Dr. Samuel Prescott, who had been in Lexington on a romantic errand, escaped to carry the news that the British were out. Several hours later the survivors of the "battle" on Lexington Green brought the news that blood had been spilled. One rider, Israel Bissel, his horse lathered

and exhausted, galloped into Worcester and cried "To arms! To arms! The war has begun!" as his horse fell dead.

In response to these alarms, militia companies from the surrounding counties shouldered arms and headed for Concord. By seven o'clock, when the British column neared the town, some 400 militiamen were there ahead of them. One company of about 150 colonials under Captain William Smith marched his men out on the road to Lexington, but upon sighting the approaching British column, he faced them about and returned to Concord where they occupied a low ridge north of the town (1). Recognizing the strategic importance of that ridge, Colonel Smith threw out his light infantry to sweep it of hostile forces. A few Americans wanted to make a stand there, but the majority called for withdrawal, and this was a genuinely democratic armed force. They fell back over the North Bridge across the Concord River to Punktasset Hill (2).

Upon entering the town, Colonel Smith divided his command into three groups. He sent three

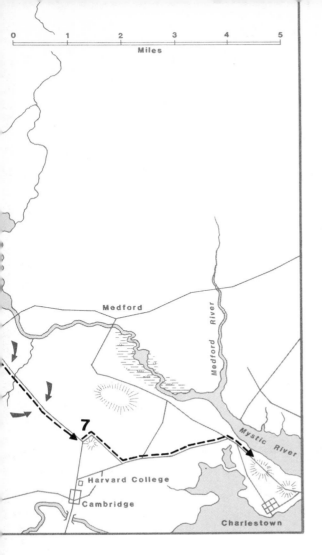

whizzed past the ear of one and he angrily cried out: "God damn it! They're firing ball!" The Americans returned fire and with their first volley twelve redcoats fell to the ground —four of them officers — and Laurie gave the order to retreat.

With possession of the bridge, the Americans had cut off the three British companies at Barrett's farm. But Colonel Barrett notwithstanding, the Americans lacked effective central command and instead of holding the bridge, they divided into two groups; about half returned to the north side of the river to gather up the bodies of their fallen comrades (2 killed and 2 wounded), and the rest returned to the ridge they had previously occupied north of town. As a result, Parson's three companies were able to slip back across the bridge and rejoin the main body.

Having fulfilled the letter of his orders, Colonel Smith decided that the time had come to return to Boston. At mid-day he reformed his command and started back down the road to Lexington. But the real battle was just beginning. At Meriam's Corner (4) the British fired into a group of American militia; the militia returned fire, and from that point on the road back to Lexington became a gauntlet of nearly constant fire as Americans sniped at the redcoats from ambush. Occasionally British flanking troops would sweep through the woods to trap a party of Americans against the road, but such maneuvers slowed the march and for most of the long day the British simply tramped along and endured the fire. Many of their dead and wounded had to be abandoned; unit cohesiveness broke down. By the time the column reached Lexington (5), the British were on the verge of complete disintegration.

At Lexington Smith's beleaguered and exhausted men were met by a relief column under Brigadier General Hugh Percy — the reinforcements that Smith had requested soon after beginning his march that morning — and its arrival probably saved Smith's command. Percy had nearly 1,000 men and he had brought artillery. The six pound balls crashing into the woods temporarily drove off the militia. For an hour the exhausted British rested, "their tongues hanging out of their mouths, like those of dogs after a chase" according to one witness, and then they resumed the march to Boston.

Around Menotomy (6) the attacks began again and took on a new fierceness. Frustrated by their ordeal, the British had begun to loot roadside homes, and angered by this barbarity, some militia units charged from the woods to grapple with the British hand to hand. Near Cambridge (7) the Americans finally broke off their attacks and the British escaped into Charlestown. They had marched over 35 miles in twenty hours, the last ten of them under fire. They had lost 273 men out of a total of 1,800 (including Percy's relief force) and the Americans 95 out of perhaps 3,500 or more. Open warfare had begun. It was a disastrous day for British arms, and for Gage's policy.

companies of light infantry under Captain Parsons across the North Bridge past Punktasset Hill toward the farm of the American militia commander, Colonel James Barrett, where cannon and other arms were reported to be hidden (3). He posted another three companies under Captain Laurie at the bridge itself to keep a wary eye on the American militiamen, and he ordered the grenadiers to search the buildings in the town for other hidden stores. In their enthusiasm the grenadiers set fire to the courthouse and a blacksmith shop and the rising smoke convinced the militiamen on Punktasset Hill that the town was about to be burned to the ground. Angry men asked Barrett if they were to stand by and allow such a thing, and Barrett gave the order to advance, but he warned his followers not to fire unless fired upon.

About 400 undisciplined militia marched down the hill and toward the three companies of British light infantrymen at the North Bridge. The British opened fire on the advancing horde, but their initial volley was so poorly aimed that the militiamen thought they were firing powder only. Then a shot

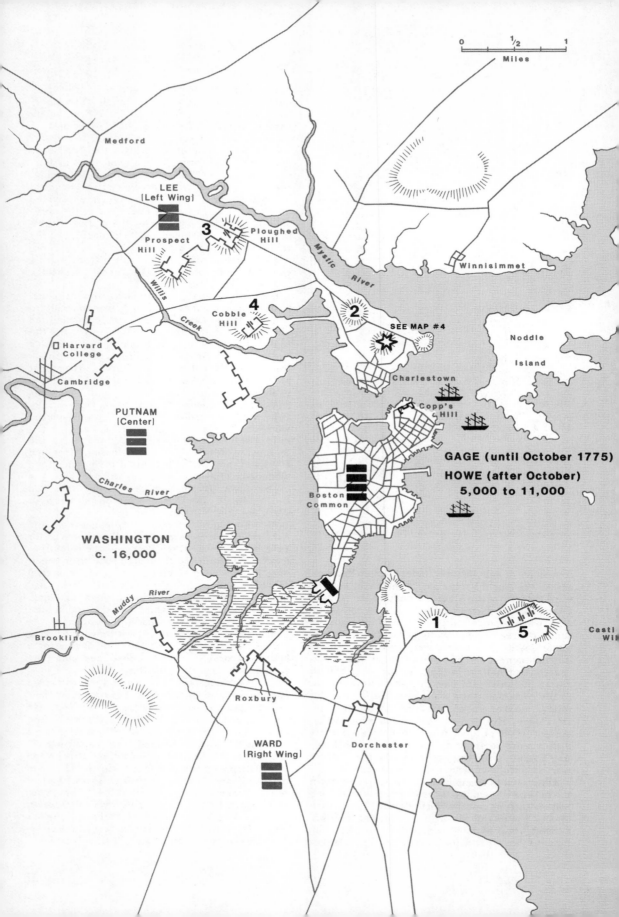

0   1/2   1
Miles

Medford

LEE
[Left Wing]

3   Ploughed
Hill

Prospect
Hill

Willis

Mystic River

Winnisimmet

4   Cobble
Hill

2

SEE MAP #4

Creek

Noddle
Island

Harvard
College

Charlestown

Cambridge

Copp's
Hill

PUTNAM
[Center]

GAGE (until October 1775)

HOWE (after October)
5,000 to 11,000

Charles River

Boston
Common

WASHINGTON
c. 16,000

Muddy River

Brookline

1

5

Castl
Wil

Roxbury

WARD
[Right Wing]

Dorchester

MAP # 3

The Siege of Boston

April, 1775-March, 1776

The British in Boston were relatively secure from a direct assault, but they were also effectively cut off from the surrounding countryside. The peculiar geography of Boston ensured that an overland attack by either side would face a Thermopylae-like defense at Boston Neck. The British might have attempted an amphibious foray out of the city, for Gage did have naval forces, but the expedition to Concord had made him cautious.

For their part, the Americans had no naval forces and were ill-equipped for an assault or even for a proper siege. For the first several months, there was no overall commander or any real organization. General Artemas Ward led the Massachusetts troops and since his was by far the largest contingent, the leaders of the other militia units generally deferred to him. But he was hardly in command. The Americans had adequate small arms since they had brought their own, but their weapons were of no uniformity and they were desperately short of powder and ball. They had little artillery, and there was no logistical organization to feed the army or to ensure the most basic hygiene. Moreover, the American milita had come as volunteers and from day to day the American commanders could never be sure how many men they had. Nevertheless, their numbers grew and by mid-summer some 15,000 to 18,000 rebels encircled the 6,500-man British garrison.

On May 25 the frigate HMS *Cerberus* arrived in Boston Harbor and deposited three British Major Generals — William Howe, Henry Clinton, and John Burgoyne — on Long Wharf. Their presence as advisors to Gage was a sure sign that London was not pleased. The three generals were shocked to find the British garrison held hostage by a provincial rabble, and they urged Gage to take action. In particular they advised him to land forces on Dorchester Neck and fortify Dorchester Heights (1). From there British forces would command the harbor and the position could also serve as a bridgehead for a subsequent British offensive. But news of British plans for such an expedition leaked and led the Americans to set in motion a plan of their own to fortify not only Dorchester Heights, but also Bunker Hill on the Charlestown peninsula (2). This fateful decision led to the Battle for Bunker Hill (see MAP # 4).

The Battle of Bunker Hill did not end the stalemate in Boston Harbor; indeed the siege was to last another eight months. But the arrival in Cambridge of George Washington two weeks afterward marked a new professionalism in the American effort. Washington immediately began to impose order on the American army. He designated badges of rank, established a logistical organization, and divided the army into three wings, each commanded by a major general. Artemas Ward commanded the largest wing covering the overland exit from Boston through Roxbury. Israel Putnam of Connecticut commanded the center from Cambridge. Charles Lee directed the left wing guarding the road out of Charlestown.

Through the late summer of 1775 both sides engaged in small raids that had little impact on the strategic situation. The Americans continued to tighten their hold on Boston by expanding their lines and building new fortifications on Ploughed Hill (3) and Cobble Hill (4), both within easy artillery range of the British redan on Bunker Hill.

Both sides suffered through the fall and winter: the British from a shortage of supplies, the Americans mostly from boredom and a shortage of warm winter quarters. The British could only complain, but many of the American militiamen voted with their feet and went home. By mid-winter Washington's army had dwindled to barely 9,000 while the British garrison had been reinforced until it actually outnumbered its besiegers. Washington's principal hope now was to make the British position in Boston untenable by establishing a battery on Dorchester Heights. In November he had dispatched Colonel Henry Knox to Fort Ticonderoga with orders to bring as many pieces of artillery as possible, and in late January the resourceful Knox returned with a full artillery train, his men having dragged the guns on sledges over the winter snows.

On March 2 the Americans began a diversionary bombardment of British positions from Cobble Hill and Ploughed Hill while an American work party erected a fortification on Dorchester Heights completing most of it in a single night. Because the ground was frozen, they erected gabions to create an above-ground breastwork (5). When the British spotted the new battery the next morning, they realized immediately the seriousness of the threat. Major General William Howe, who had replaced Gage in October, ordered an attack on the new American position, but a severe storm on the night of March 4 gave him an excuse to call it off. Howe had planned to evacuate Boston soon in any case and he did not want to risk another Bunker Hill. On March 17, after an eleven-month siege, the British evacuated the city and sailed to Halifax.

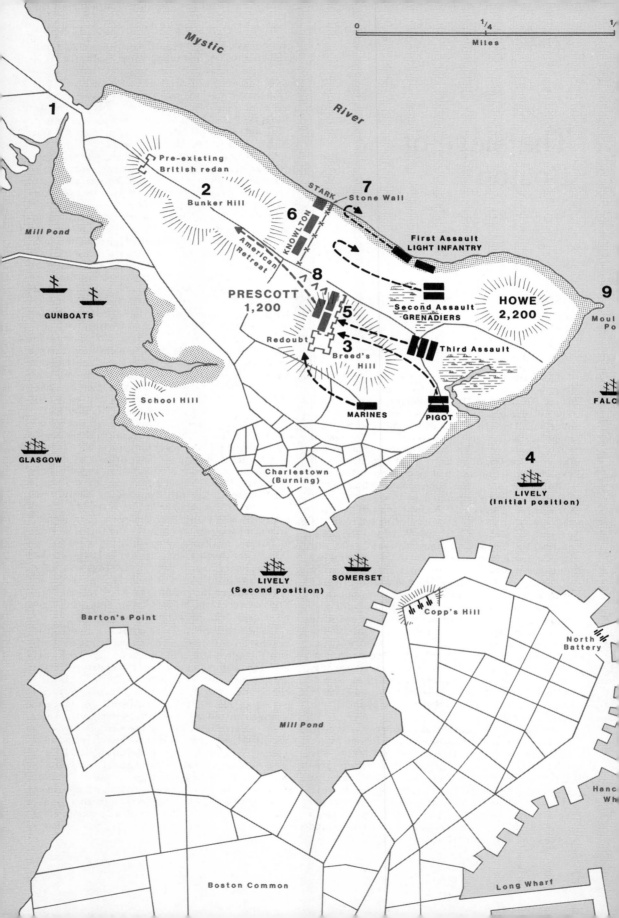

Mystic

River

Mill Pond

1

Pre-existing
British redan

Bunker Hill

2

STARK

7

Stone Wall

6

KNOWLTON

First Assault
LIGHT INFANTRY

American
Retreat

8

Second Assault
GRENADIERS

**HOWE
2,200**

9

**PRESCOTT
1,200**

5

Moul
Po

Redoubt

3

Breed's
Hill

Third Assault

GUNBOATS

School Hill

MARINES

PIGOT

FALC

GLASGOW

4

**LIVELY
(Initial position)**

Charlestown
(Burning)

LIVELY
(Second position)

SOMERSET

Barton's Point

Copp's Hill

North
Battery

Mill Pond

Hanc
Wh

Boston Common

Long Wharf

0   1/4   1/
Miles

MAP # 4

Bunker Hill

June 17, 1775

At six p.m. on June 16 just over 1000 men assembled in the American camp at Cambridge and marched to the Charlestown Neck (1) where for the first time they were told their mission: to erect a fortification and a battery on Bunker Hill (2). Typically they got into a discussion about whether it would be better to fortify Breed's Hill (3), which was closer to Boston but some 35 feet lower in height, rather than Bunker Hill. In the end they decided, again typically, to compromise: they would fortify Breed's Hill first, then Bunker Hill. Colonel Richard Gridley laid out the plan for a small redoubt on Breed's Hill and at about midnight the Americans finally set to work with pick and shovel. At four a.m., dawn exposed their work to the British warships and HMS *Lively* (4) opened fire.

The British cannonade did little damage but it unnerved the amateur soldiers in the American redoubt. To calm them, the American commander, Colonel William Prescott, made a point of flaunting the British bombardment by pacing about atop the unfinished "fort." From his vantage point the growing dawn showed him just how exposed his men were on Breed's Hill. He immediately ordered some of them to begin constructing an additional breastwork to the north (5) and asked for reinforcements. He sent Captain Thomas Knowlton's 300 men to a rail fence on his left flank (6), and John Stark's regiment occupied the narrow beach below the rail fence where his men built a breastwork of stones (7). In the gap between the breastwork and the rail fence, the Americans built three small fleches, small field works with only two faces (8).

Across Boston Harbor, the British quadrumvirate of generals debated. Clinton argued for a landing on Charlestown neck in the rear of the American redoubt, but Gage noted that such a move would put British soldiers between two enemy forces. They decided instead to land on Moulton's Point (9) and advance along the Mystic River to take the American redoubt in the flank and rear. Some 1500 men were selected for this assignment; another 700 were to be held in reserve. Howe was to command. The British forces embarked at Long Wharf and North Battery and landed on Moulton's Point at 1 p.m. Only from Moulton's Hill did Howe see the breastwork that Prescott had added since daylight. He decided to send for the reserves at once.

Howe's plan to turn the rebel left depended on the success of the eleven companies of light infantry that he directed against Stark's men on the narrow sandy beach along the Mystic River. The light infantry advanced at a steady pace unencumbered by the high grass, boggy ground, and fences that slowed the advance of the grenadiers above them on the higher ground. They marched four-abreast toward the low stone wall where Colonel John Stark's men were lined up three deep. The Americans waited until the British were within fifty yards — optimum effective range with their muskets — and then they poured a volley into the head of the column. The British infantrymen fell in droves and the beach became clogged with dead and dying soldiers. The British could not fire back for Howe had ordered them to rely on their bayonets and their muskets were unloaded. As the men in the front ranks fell, the men further back in the column pushed ahead, and the front of the column melted away like a candle pressed against a hot plate. Finally they could bear no more and the column stopped, turned, and fled back down the beach. Ninety-six dead British soldiers littered the beach. They were as thick, said one American, as sheep in a fold. Howe's flanking movement had failed.

Deciding that the narrow defile along the beach denied him the opportunity to take advantage of his superior numbers, Howe determined to direct the second assault against the rail fence. At the same time, Colonel Robert Pigot was to attack the breastwork and the main redoubt. In this attack the British ranks were again blasted by accurate American musket fire at close range and again they fell back. Howe now realized that he faced the possibility of actual defeat. If he launched a third attack and it failed, he believed he could not ask the men to try a fourth time. He sent for the last of his reserves — some 400 men from Boston — and ordered all his men, finally, to discard their heavy packs. This third, and final, attack would be concentrated against the breastwork and the fort itself.

The determined British drove up the hill into the teeth of the American fire. By now the Americans were running out of ammunition — some had resorted to throwing rocks — and the British would not be denied. Only when the British were inside the fort and the fighting was hand-to-hand did Prescott finally give the order to retreat. The British attempted a pursuit, but they were exhausted, and Knowlton's soldiers at the rail fence provided a steady covering fire while withdrawing in good order.. Altogether some 1,054 British soldiers fell killed or wounded compared to 440 American casualties. Clinton provided the most appropriate assessment: "A dear bought victory, another such would have ruined us."

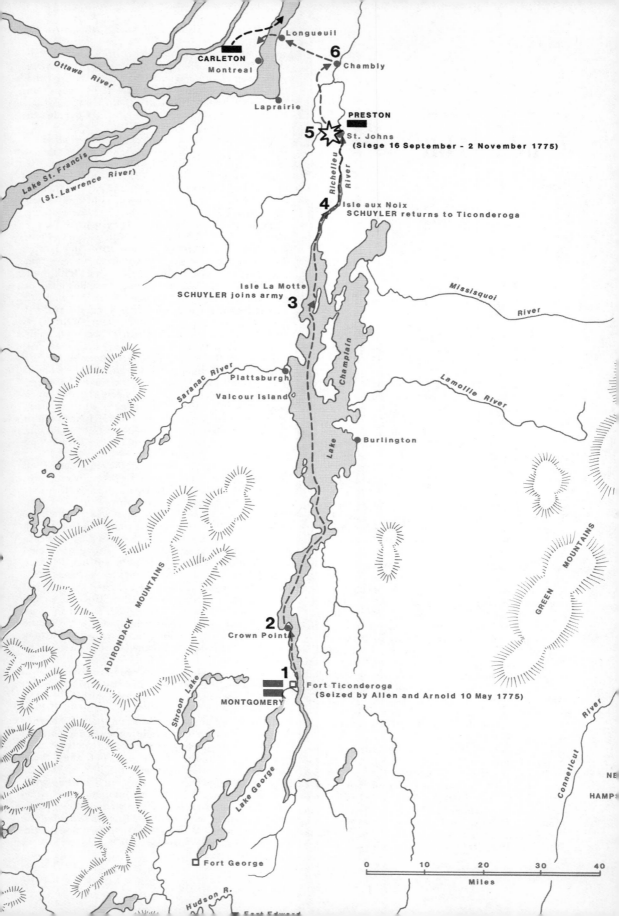

Ottawa River

Longueuil

CARLETON
Montreal

Lake St. Francis

(St. Lawrence River)

Laprairie

Chambly

6

PRESTON

5 St. Johns
(Siege 16 September – 2 November 1775)

Richelieu River

4 Isle aux Noix
SCHUYLER returns to Ticonderoga

Isle La Motte
SCHUYLER joins army **3**

Missisquoi River

Saranac River
Plattsburgh

Valcour Island

Lake Champlain

Lamoille River

Burlington

GREEN MOUNTAINS

ADIRONDACK MOUNTAINS

Schroon Lake

2
Crown Point

Connecticut River

NE
HAMP

1 Fort Ticonderoga
(Seized by Allen and Arnold 10 May 1775)

MONTGOMERY

Lake George

Fort George

| 0 | 10 | 20 | 30 | 40 |
Miles

Hudson R.

Fort Edward

MAP # 5

American Invasion of Canada

August-November, 1775

In the spring of 1775, during the early stages of the American siege of Boston, the Continental Congress in Philadelphia invited the Canadian provinces to join in their resistance to British "tyranny." The Canadians were cool to the idea and Congress was not of a mind to push it. But Ethan Allen, leader of the Green Mountain Boys, and Benedict Arnold were. Both men had participated in the seizure of Fort Ticonderoga (1) in May and they saw it as a springboard for a northward invasion. On June 27, partly in response to Allen's lobbying, Congress authorized aggressive action if it seemed practicable and was not disagreeable to the Canadians. An important factor in the American decision was the threat posed by Colonel Guy Johnson, the British Indian agent in Canada, who was attempting to stir up the northern Indians against the Colonials.

The traditional north-south invasion route between Canada and the English colonies was the waterway formed by Lake Champlain and Lake George. Champlain connected with the St. Lawrence by the Richelieu River flowing northward, and the head of Lake George was only a few wilderness miles from the Hudson River which flowed south to New York. This natural water highway had been used by both sides in the colonial wars between England and France and each had built forts along it.

Major General Philip Schuyler, who commanded American Continental forces in New York state, arrived at Ticonderoga on July 28 to find his command in a deplorable state of readiness. Though the Americans had about twice as many men under arms as the British, they were all untested militiamen and Schuyler himself, though a capable administrator, was in poor health and as uncertain of his own well-being as he was of the mettle of his soldiers. Schuyler's second in command at Ticonderoga was Brigadier General Richard Montgomery whose youth, enthusiasm, and good health all contrasted markedly with his commander.

In late July, while Schuyler was away attending a council of war, Montgomery heard rumors that the British were building a major naval combatant at St. Johns. On his own, he ordered the American army, grown now to some 1,500, to advance. He headed northward down the lake to Crown Point (2) and then on to Isle La Motte (3). Schuyler rejoined the army there on September 4 and that day the American flotilla of one schooner, one sloop and some gondolas headed northward again for Isle aux Noix (4) in the Richelieu River. The next day the Americans advanced down the Richelieu toward the British fort at St. Johns (5) commanded by Sir Charles Preston.

Outside St. Johns American scouts so exaggerated the strength of the St. Johns garrison that Schuyler lost his nerve and ordered a retreat back to Isle aux Noix. He tried again on September 10, but this "attack" proved equally futile, and indeed almost embarrassing. Converging columns of American soldiers collided in the dark and both groups turned and fled. After this fiasco, Schuyler decided that he was too ill to continue the campaign and he returned to Ticonderoga leaving Montgomery in command.

On September 16 Montgomery returned to St. Johns and this time the Americans established a regular siege. In addition Montgomery sent several delegates, including the mercurial Ethan Allen, northward to recruit Canadian volunteers whom the Americans were convinced were eager to join the rebellion. Allen and Major John Brown gathered some 300 followers, but instead of returning to the American camp around St. Johns, they decided to seize the lightly-defended city of Montreal. Allen crossed the St. Lawrence downriver from Montreal on the night of September 24, but Brown's forces never showed up. The next day Carleton sent 250 militia volunteers to oppose Allen's men. The latter were not expecting a fight; they fired one volley and fled. Allen and 35 others were captured.

Meanwhile the operations at St. Johns continued. Rain and a shortage of supplies created disheartening conditions for the besiegers. To break the impasse, Montgomery sent 50 Americans and 300 sympathetic Canadians northward in October to seize the British outpost at Chambly (6) which was defended by a small 88 man garrison commanded by Major Joseph Stopford. Preston's communications with Montreal were cut, and he surrendered St. Johns on November 2.

Montgomery was eager to exploit his success despite the lateness of the season. Some of his men were unenthusiastic about prolonging the campaign into the winter months and Montgomery had to bully or cajole them into make another advance. Nevertheless, the Americans arrived on the banks of the St. Lawrence River above Montreal on November 12 and Carleton, who had only about 150 men under arms, evacuated the city. Two days later Montreal formally surrendered. Carleton escaped to Quebec, the last British stronghold on the St. Lawrence and the next American target.

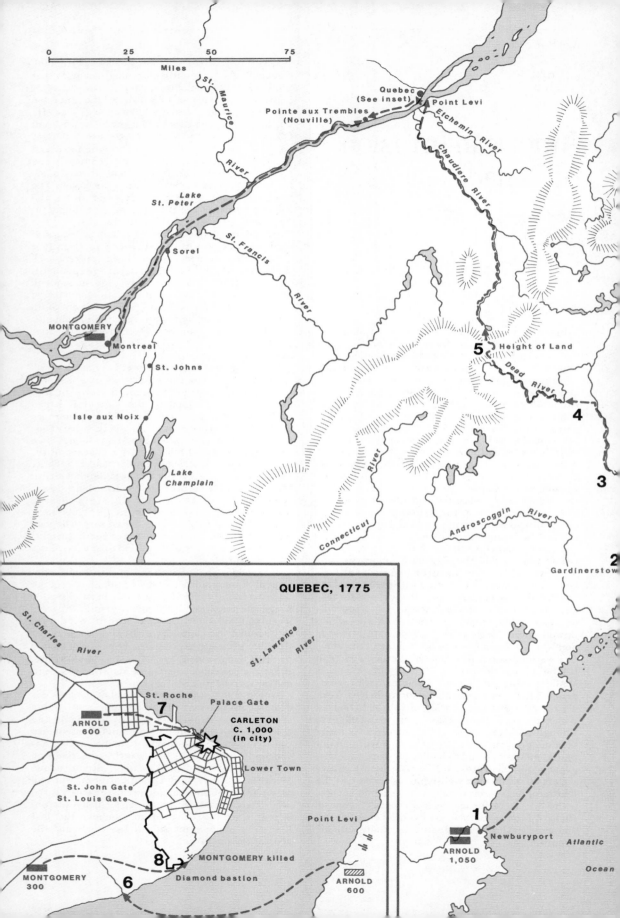

0   25   50   75
Miles

St. Maurice River

Quebec
(See inset)
Point Levi

Pointe aux Trembles
(Nouville)

Etchemin River

Chaudiere River

Lake
St. Peter

St. Francis River

Sorel

5   Height of Land

Dead River

4

MONTGOMERY

Montreal

St. Johns

3

Isle aux Noix

Lake
Champlain

Connecticut River

Androscoggin River

2

Gardinerstow

QUEBEC, 1775

St. Charles River

St. Lawrence River

St. Roche

Palace Gate

7

**CARLETON
C. 1,000
(in city)**

ARNOLD
600

Lower Town

St. John Gate
St. Louis Gate

Point Levi

1

Newburyport

Atlantic

Ocean

ARNOLD
1,050

8   MONTGOMERY killed

MONTGOMERY
300

6   Diamond bastion

ARNOLD
600

MAP # 6

Arnold's March to Quebec

September-December, 1775

In June of 1775 Benedict Arnold resigned his disputed command at Ticonderoga and petitioned Congress for another. In August Washington offered him the command of an expedition against the Canadian citadel of Quebec. Arnold accepted with his customary enthusiasm and his small army of some 1,050 sailed from Newburyport (1) on September 19. It landed three days later at Gardinerstown (2) where Arnold had arranged for 200 bateaux — double ended flat bottomed boats — to meet him.

Arnold's route had been previously surveyed and was advertised to be nearly as passable as Montgomery's Lake Champlain-Lake George route. But in fact the Kenebec River and the small series of streams that "connected" it to the Chaudière on the other side of the height-of-land were narrow, dangerous, and dotted alternately with rapids and swamps which required the men to carry their heavy bateaux for miles through absolute wilderness. Expecting a boat ride, Arnold's men would instead confront one of the most harrowing wilderness treks in history.

Trouble began almost at once. On October 6 they had to portage around Norridgewock Falls (3). This took three days, but was only a foretaste of things to come. Two days later the expedition arrived at the "Great Carrying Place" (4). By the time the boats had been manhandled over this barrier onto the ominously-named Dead River, the expedition had taken more time than Arnold had allotted to the entire journey. Moreover, the Dead River, though calm on the surface, flowed against them with a strong current; the men had to hug the banks and pull the boats along with their hands. On October 19 it began to rain and three days later it was still raining. The Dead River overflowed its banks and the entire countryside became a shallow lake. The men slogged ahead on foot through knee deep water in bitter cold. On October 25 Lieutenant Colonel Roger Enos' division of some 300 men voted to turn back.

At the height-of-land (5), the Americans abandoned their bateaux and clawed and stumbled their way four and a half miles over the rough trail across the mountains. Finally they reached the Chaudière. But they were now completely out of food and survived only by eating moccasins, shot pouches, and soap. Finally on November 2 they met an advance party returning with fresh meat and flour. Of the nearly 1,100 men who began the march, some 400 had turned back, and as many as a hundred more had died along the way. Only about 600 were left to meet the advance party. On November 9 this remnant arrived at Point Levi opposite Quebec (see inset).

Though the garrison of Quebec consisted of only about 70 regulars, Carleton could muster several hundred militia and the soldiers and marines from two British warships in the river — a total of perhaps 1000-1200. Arnold's 600 were worn out, low on powder, and without artillery. Arnold was nevertheless determined to make an attempt to seize the city. The Americans ferried across the river in canoes on the night of November 13 disembarking at the same landing site that Wolfe had used in his conquest of Quebec in 1759 (6). Arnold at first established his camp only a mile or two away from the city walls, but news that the British planned a sortie led him to pull back some 20 miles to Pointe aux Trembles.

On December 2 Richard Montgomery arrived in Arnold's camp at the head of 300 men from Montreal. Prompted by expiring enlistments, the two American commanders planned an attack against the lightly fortified Lower Town. Arnold would lead his 600 men along the edge of the St. Charles River from the suburb of St. Roche (7), and Montgomery would take his 300 along the narrow path at the foot of Cape Diamond south of the city (8). They would wait for a dark night to make the attempt.

Their opportunity came on New Year's Eve, 1775. Arnold's men made it past the Palace Gate barricade but stalled at a barricade Carleton had thrown up across the Sault au Matelot, the main street into the Lower Town. In the early skirmishing, Arnold was wounded in the leg and had to be carried to the rear. Captain Daniel Morgan assumed command of the street fighting that ensued. Carleton sent a column of 200 men to cut off the American retreat. Unless Montgomery's detachment arrived soon, the Americans would have to capitulate.

Montgomery at that moment lay dead in the snow at the foot of Cape Diamond. Leading the advance guard along the narrow path by the river, he had been killed by the first British volley. Disheartened, the rest of his command turned back. Morgan's men held out until dawn when they finally surrendered. Carleton captured 426 Americans; another 60 or so had been killed or wounded. British losses totaled only five killed and thirteen wounded.

The Americans maintained a desultory "siege" through the winter, but on May 6, 1775 a British squadron with reinforcements arrived at Quebec. That same morning Carleton sortied against the discouraged American besiegers who abandoned their guns and equipment and fled to Montreal.

23

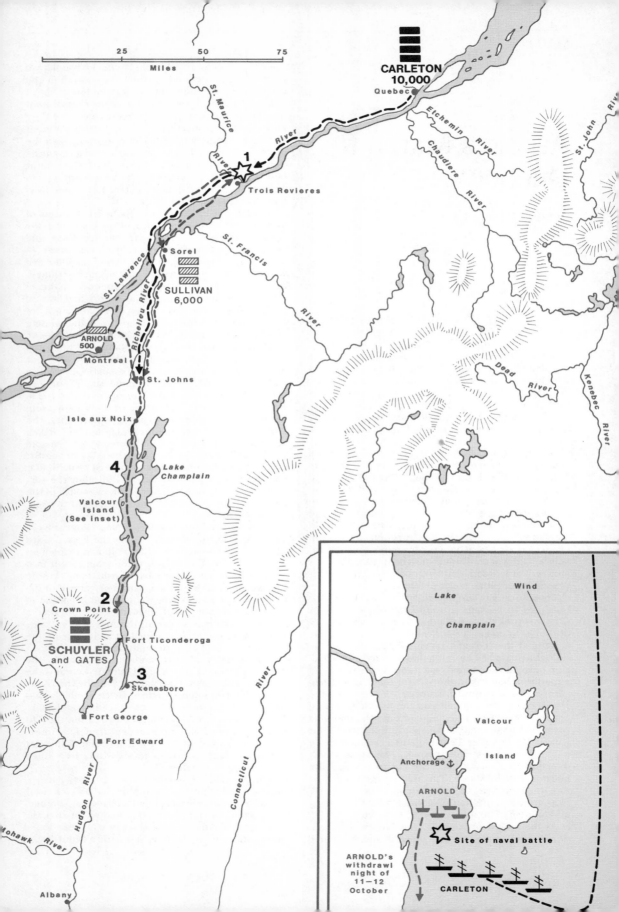

CARLETON
10,000

25   50   75

Miles

St. Maurice

River

St. Maurice

River

Quebec

Etchemin River

Chaudiere River

St. John River

1

Trois Revieres

Sorel

St. Francis

River

SULLIVAN
6,000

St. Lawrence

Richelieu River

ARNOLD
500

Montreal

St. Johns

Isle aux Noix

Dead

River

Kenebec

River

4

Lake
Champlain

Valcour
Island
(See inset)

2

Crown Point

Connecticut

River

SCHUYLER
and GATES

Fort Ticonderoga

3

Skenesboro

Fort George

Fort Edward

Hudson River

Mohawk River

Albany

Lake

Champlain

Wind

Valcour

Island

Anchorage

ARNOLD

Site of naval battle

ARNOLD's
withdrawl
night of
11—12
October

CARLETON

MAP # 7

Valcour Island

October 11, 1776

More British reinforcements arrived at Quebec on June 1: nine regiments of British regulars and some 3,000 German mercenaries under the command of Major General Baron von Riedesel, giving Carleton a total strength of nearly 11,000. The Americans at Montreal had also been reinforced. Brigadier General John Sullivan, the new American commander, brought four fresh regiments of Continentals from Albany, but Sullivan's enthusiastic optimism was altogether inappropriate to the new situation. He ordered an attack on the British advance guard at Trois Riviéres (1) on June 8, but his columns became separated in the swamps and thick woods; outnumbered and outmaneuvered, they fled upriver.

Despite this fiasco, Sullivan remained determined to hold Sorel and defend upper Canada to the last extremity, but cooler heads prevailed. Benedict Arnold, commanding at Montreal, wrote him: "The junction of the Canadas is now at an end. Let us quit them and secure our own country before it is too late." The Americans fell back all the way to Crown Point (2) where they were able to concentrate nearly as many men — on paper — as the British. But defeat and disease — especially smallpox and malaria — ruined their morale. They lacked adequate shelter, clothing, and provisions. John Adams reported to Congress that "Our army at Crown Point is an object of wretchedness to fill a humane mind with horror; disgraced, defeated, discontented, diseased, naked, undisciplined, eaten up with vermin; no clothes, beds, blankets, no medicines; no victuals, but salt pork and flour." This miserable force was all that stood between the British and the traditional invasion route up Lake Champlain into the heart of New York. The Congressional response to this crisis was the appointment on June 17 of Major General Horatio Gates to replace Sullivan. Gates remained under the overall command of Philip Schuyler.

The key to stopping the British advance was command of Lake Champlain. Aware of this, the British undertook the construction of a fleet at St. Johns. Carleton ordered that the ship-rigged *Inflexible* with its 18 guns be dismantled on the St.

Lawrence and carried overland in sections to be reassembled on the lake. In addition the British built two schooners (of 14 and 12 guns respectively), a gondola (7 guns), some twenty gunboats, and a giant raft-like vessel called a *radeau* which carried heavy 24 pounders and a crew of 300, and which was appropriately named *Thunderer*. To confront this armada, the Americans had only four small vessels mounting a total of 36 guns. Recognizing the inadequacy of this squadron, Gates authorized Benedict Arnold to supervise the construction of as many new warships as he could put together.

By offering special pay, Arnold gathered together craftsmen of all types —blacksmiths, riggers, and sailmakers — at Skenesboro (3) and put Brigadier General David Waterbury in charge of construction. Through July and August the Americans built a half dozen gundalows (flat-bottomed single-masted vessels carrying 3 guns and a crew of 45), and an equal number of galleys (somewhat larger vessels with 8 to 10 guns and a crew of 70 to 80). By the end of August, Arnold was sailing northward to challenge the British for control of the lake.

Through September Arnold remained in the vicinity of Bay St. Ann above Cumberland Head (4) drilling his green crews in the curiosities of their strange craft — themselves built mostly of green wood. On October 11 lookouts spotted the British fleet moving southward up the lake. Carleton's ships had passed Valcour Island (see inset) before Carleton realized that the American fleet was lurking in its lee. To attack, Carleton had to beat back against the wind. Not all of his vessels were able to close, and the ungainly *Thunderer* played no part in the battle. The schooner *Carleton* took the brunt of the American fire and had to be towed out of danger by British gunboats. But the fire of the *Inflexible* overpowered the smaller American vessels, though darkness fell before the British could complete their victory.

The Americans were in a desperate situation. The wind pinned them into the channel between Valcour Island and the western shore of the lake with the British battleline stretched across their line of retreat. Nevertheless, in the dark and fog of the early morning hours, the American vessels assembled in line-ahead formation and slipped past the British. Carleton pursued the next morning and soon caught up with the smaller and slower American ships. Arnold fought a running rear guard battle until he was forced to beach his ships and set them afire to prevent their falling to the British. Only five American vessels made it to Crown Point.

Arnold lost 11 of his 16 vessels and, more importantly, he lost command of Lake Champlain. But his energy in challenging the British for command of the lake had forced a naval action that, however one-sided, was nevertheless of crucial importance to American victory. For with command of the lake, Charleton decided after the battle that it was too late in the season to continue the campaign. He withdrew to St. Johns to await the spring.

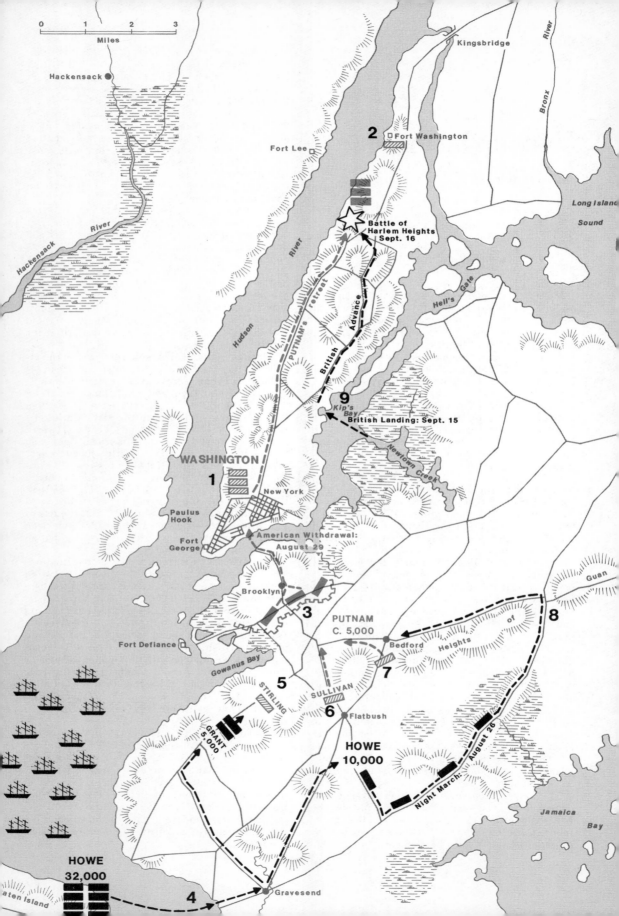

Miles
0 1 2 3

Hackensack

Kingsbridge

Bronx River

Hackensack River

Fort Lee

2 Fort Washington

Long Island Sound

Hudson River

Battle of
Harlem Heights
Sept. 16

Hell's Gate

PUTNAM's retreat

British Advance

9
Kip's Bay
British Landing: Sept. 15

Newtown Creek

WASHINGTON

1

New York

Paulus
Hook

Fort George

American Withdrawal:
August 29

Brooklyn

3

PUTNAM
C. 5,000

Bedford

Heights

Guan

8

of

Fort Defiance

7

Gowanus Bay

5

STIRLING

SULLIVAN

6 Flatbush

HOWE
10,000

Night March:
August 26

GRANT
5,000

Jamaica
Bay

HOWE
32,000

4

Gravesend

aten Island

MAP # 8

New York, I: Long Island and Harlem Heights

August, 1776

In late June of 1776 while the Americans retreated from Canada, the first elements of a virtual British armada entered lower New York Harbor and began disgorging troops onto Staten Island. For weeks the British fleet grew in size until by mid-July ten ships of the line, twenty frigates, and nearly three hundred transports and supply vessels choked lower New York Harbor, their bare masts resembling a forest stripped of its leaves, according to one observer. General William Howe commanded the 32,000-man army, and his brother, Admiral Sir Richard Howe, commanded the escorting fleet. London had decided to take the war seriously.

To confront this impressive force, Washington had only about 19,000 soldiers, though reinforcements through the summer raised his total to 28,000 by August. This numerical imbalance was aggravated by the fact that the Americans had no naval forces at all, and Washington was painfully aware that he could be outflanked by sea almost anywhere in the New York area. But New York City had tremendous political significance and Washington believed he could not abandon it without a fight. He therefore divided his army into five divisions, placing three of them in New York City at the southern tip of Manhattan Island (1), one at Fort Washington near the northern end of the island (2), and one under General Nathaniel Greene on Long Island to protect Brooklyn Heights (3) which, since it overlooked the city, was the key to New York. Alas for American fortunes, Greene fell ill and his second in command, John Sullivan, was junior to Israel Putnam, who assumed command. This was an unfortunate development for though Putnam had plenty of courage, he was not an effective senior commander.

On August 22 Howe landed some 15,000 soldiers — about half his force — at Gravesend Bay on Long Island (4). The key geographical feature on Long Island was the long narow ridge running roughly east-west known as the Heights of Guan. It was pierced by four passes: Gowanus Road (5), Flatbush Road (6), Bedford Pass (7), and Jamaica Pass (8). Howe feinted against both Flatbush and Bedford Passes and Putnam accordingly positioned most of his available troops there. Then on the night of August 26, Howe's main body of 10,000 men marched uncontested through Jamaica Pass. Sullivan's badly outnumbered forces at Bedford Pass and Flatbush Pass broke and fled for the fortified American camp around Brooklyn.

While Howe led the British main body through Jamaica Pass, the rest of Howe's force — some 5,000 men under Major General James Grant — assaulted Gowanus Pass. Grant's job was to hold the 1,600 Americans under Major General William Alexander, who claimed an Irish title as Lord Stirling, in their positions until Howe could attack them in the flank and rear. Accordingly Grant was very tentative in his advance and he convinced Putnam to keep Stirling's men in the closing trap. Putnam never really comprehended the developing situation. As a result, Stirling's men were pinned between two forces of nearly ten times their number, and forced to capitulate.

Recognizing potential disaster, Washington crossed the East River from New York and assumed direct command of the demoralized American force on Long Island. He knew that New York City could not be held without possession of Brooklyn Heights, and that Brooklyn Heights could be cut off by the Royal Navy. The only sensible recourse was to abandon the city, but he was unwilling to do that. He called for more reinforcements from Manhattan to boost American strength on Long Island to 9,500, still only about half the strength of the British.

Howe was now in a position to bag most of the Continental Army and its commander with it. But perhaps remembering the results of his hasty assault at Bunker Hill, he instead began constructing regular siege lines. Heavy rains slowed his progress, and in the interval provided by nature, Washington began to appreciate just how precarious his situation was. Finally on August 29 he ordered a retreat. That night, in six hours of heavy labor, all 9,500 men and all but six guns were successfully evacuated to Manhattan. Total American losses in the campaign for Long Island were 1,012 compared to British losses of only 392.

But the Americans had not escaped yet. On Manhattan they were still on an island facing a foe that commanded the sea. Washington posted his forces as best he could and awaited the next enemy stroke. Howe gave him plenty of time; he did not move against Manhattan until September 15 when 4,000 British troops made an amphibious landing at Kip's Bay (9) thus cutting Putnam's division in New York City off from the rest of the American army near Harlem Heights. Putnam abandoned his guns and marched northward to join the main body.

In the Battle of Harlem Heights (September 16), the Americans won a sharp stand-up fight against the British regulars inflicting some 270 casualties, while accepting only half as many. This American success breathed new life into the dispirited army and caused Howe, once again, to pause.

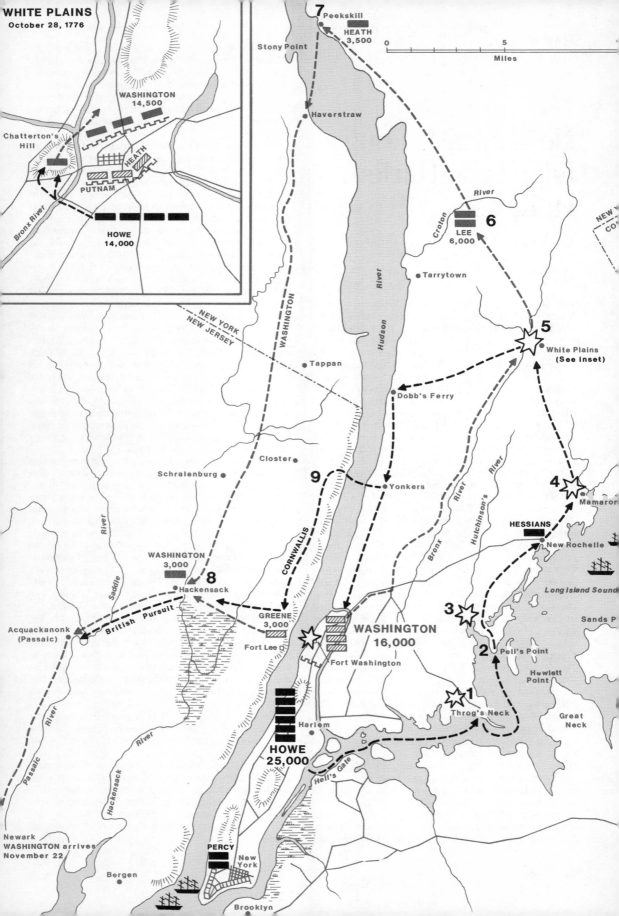

WHITE PLAINS
October 28, 1776

WASHINGTON 14,500

Chatterton's Hill

HEATH

PUTNAM

Bronx River

HOWE 14,000

0   5
                Miles

7 Peekskill
HEATH
3,500

Stony Point

Haverstraw

River

Croton

6

LEE
6,000

Tarrytown

Hudson River

NEW
CO

NEW YORK
NEW JERSEY

Tappan

Dobb's Ferry

White Plains
(See inset)

5

WASHINGTON

9

Closter

Schralenburg

Yonkers

Hutchinson's River

4

Mamaron

HESSIANS

New Rochelle

Long Island Sound

Sands P

Saddle River

WASHINGTON
3,000

8

Hackensack

CORNWALLIS

Bronx River

Acquackanonk
(Passaic)

British Pursuit

GREENE
3,000

Fort Lee

WASHINGTON
16,000

3

2 Pell's Point

Howlett
Point

Passaic River

Fort Washington

1

Throg's Neck

Great
Neck

Hackensack River

Harlem

HOWE
25,000

Hell's Gate

Newark
WASHINGTON arrives
November 22

PERCY

New
York

Bergen

Brooklyn

MAP # 9

New York, II: White Plains

September-October 1776

The American victory at Harlem Heights was a tonic for Washington's soldiers, who had done little but retreat since the campaign opened. One American officer wrote home to his wife that "The men have recovered their spirits and feel a confidence which before they had quite lost."

The battle had the opposite effect on Howe. Reluctant as always to assault rebel entrenchments, he decided once again to attempt to outmaneuver his enemy. On October 12, four thousand British soldiers embarked on transports at Kip's Bay, passed through Hell's Gate, and landed on Throg's Neck (1). Strategically the movement was a good idea, but Howe could hardly have chosen a worse place to land. The neck was nearly an island separated from the mainland by a single road that ran through marshes where a small group of Pennsylvania riflemen under the command of Colonel Edward Hand held the only bridge. Howe hesitated to force a crossing and Hand's men were reinforced. After six days, Howe decided to abandon Throg's Neck and moved his forces to Pell's Point (2).

At Eastchester (3) a brigade of about 750 Americans under Colonel John Glover contested the road with Howe's 4,000 regulars. Though Glover was forced to withdraw, his men did so in good order after inflicting more casualties than they suffered. In another skirmish four days later, Colonel John Haslet's Delaware regiment attacked and mauled Colonel Robert Rogers's regiment of about 500 loyalists at Marmaroneck (4).

Howe's move threatened to cut off the American army on Manhattan from the mainland, but Washington had already decided to abandon Manhattan and lower New York and fall back to White Plains. Sensitive to Congressional urgings, however, the American commander left some 2,800 men under Colonel Robert Magaw at Fort Washington in hopes of disrupting British transit of the Hudson River. Greene, with about 3,500 men, held Fort Lee across the river in New Jersey. Washington's main army of about 14,500 arrived in White Plains (5) on October 22. Howe dallied at New Rochelle for two days, long enough to let Washington get safely to his new position. Then

when 8,000 Hessians under Lieutenant General Wilhelm von Knyphausen arrived, Howe left half of them to garrison New Rochelle and started after Washington with about 14,000 men.

A week later on October 28 the two armies met in the Battle of White Plains (see inset). Putnam held the American right, Brigadier General William Heath the left, and Washington himself the center. But the key to the position was the high ground beyond the Bronx River known as Chatterton's Hill. About 4,000 British and Hessians attacked the 1,600 Americans under Colonel Joseph Reed on Chatterton's Hill. The American militia broke and fled, but the Continentals fought stubbornly. As at Harlem Heights and Eastchester, the Americans inflicted more casualties than they suffered, but they were forced to give up the hill and its loss uncovered the American right. Washington had little choice but to withdraw northward to Castle Hill (6).

Howe, now reinforced to 20,000, did not follow. Instead he turned west to Dobb's Ferry, and then south to achieve the envelopment of Magaw's force in Fort Washington. Washington left Lee in command of about 6,000 men at Castle Hill to block any northward move by Howe, and led the rest of his army northwest to Peekskill (7). From there he crossed the Hudson at Haverstraw (on November 10) and marched south to Hackensack, New Jersey (8).

Washington's decision to divide his already inferior forces and place the Hudson River between them was a serious error in military judgement. Equally questionable was his decision to leave Magaw's 2,800 men in Fort Washington where, on November 16, they were forced to capitulate. But in this, as in other things, Washington had acted in accordance with the wishes of Congress, and it could be argued that Washington's greatest service in the war was his definition of the role of commander in chief as subordinate to Congress. The loss of Magaw's 2,800 men was an unalloyed military disaster, but the solution urged by Charles Lee — a military dictatorship (with himself as dictator) —would have been a greater disaster.

After the capitulation of Fort Washington, Howe sent Cornwallis across the Hudson at Closter (9) in an attempt to seize Fort Lee. Warned in the nick of time, Greene managed to escape, though he had to leave much valuable equipment behind. He marched his force west and joined Washington at Hackensack on November 20. With only about 3,500 effectives, half of whom were obligated only until the end of the year, Washington fled west to Acquackinonk and then southward to Newark where he arrived on November 22 with Cornwallis in pursuit.

All in all it had been a disastrous campaign. Washington lost New York City and over 4,000 men to the enemy. In battle the Americans had performed well, but despite his hesitancy, Howe had clearly outmaneuvered Washington. Finally, many of Washington's veterans were preparing to go home at the end of their enlistments in December. For the Americans, a crisis was at hand.

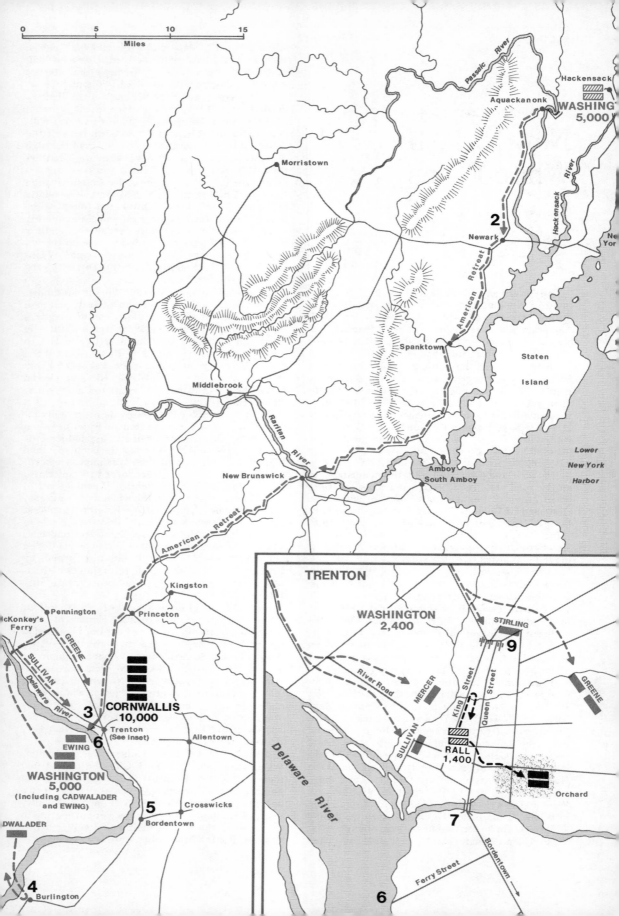

0 5 10 15
Miles

Passaic River

Hackensack

Aquackanonk

WASHING
5,000

Morristown

2

Newark

American Retreat

Spanktown

Staten
Island

Hackensack River

New Yor

Middlebrook

Raritan River

New Brunswick

Amboy
South Amboy

Lower
New York
Harbor

American Retreat

Kingston

McKonkey's
Ferry

Pennington

Princeton

GREENE

SULLIVAN

Delaware River

3

CORNWALLIS
10,000

Trenton
(See inset)

Allentown

EWING

6

WASHINGTON
5,000
(including CADWALADER
and EWING)

DWALADER

5

Crosswicks

Bordentown

4
Burlington

TRENTON

WASHINGTON
2,400

River Road

MERCER

SULLIVAN

King Street

Queen Street

STIRLING

9

GREENE

RALL
1,400

Orchard

Delaware River

7

6

Ferry Street

Bordentown

MAP # 10

Trenton

December 25, 1776

From Hackensack (1) Washington's dispirited and weary men marched southward leaving northern New Jersey to the British. Washington paused at Newark (2) hoping to hear from Charles Lee whose 6,000 men were still in New York. Washington sent Lee several urgent requests to join him, but Lee was enjoying his independent command and delayed crossing the Hudson into New Jersey until December. Meanwhile Howe entrusted the pursuit of Washington to Major General Charles Cornwallis and Washington soon discovered that Cornwallis was more aggressive than Howe. On November 28, the van of Cornwallis' troops marched into Newark as Washington's rear guard was leaving. As if the situation was not desperate enough, a few days later the enlistments of nearly half of Washington's men expired and nearly 2,000 of them left for home. With the remnant of his forces, Washington continued his flight southward to Trenton (3); his one hope was to put the Delaware River between himself and his relentless enemy.

By December 8 the two armies faced each other across the Delaware at Trenton. They represented a striking contrast: the British —10,000 strong — were well-clothed, well-equipped, well-led, and confident; the Americans, only half their number, were still in summer uniforms, many of them without shoes, short on supplies of all kinds, and greatly dispirited from the series of defeats and defections. Charles Lee continued to confound Washington with his reluctance to join the main body. Around their campfires Washington's men nodded gravely to one another when someone read aloud the opening lines of Thomas Paine's famous pamphlet published that month: "These are the times that try men's souls. . . ." But Howe again betrayed his lack of a killer instinct. On December 14 he ordered British forces into winter quarters — a string of outposts stretching from New York to Trenton. Howe himself returned to New York while Cornwallis planned a winter leave in England. As far as Howe was concerned, the campaign for the year had ended. He was wrong.

Washington's decision to counterattack at Trenton on Christmas Day of 1776 was the most audacious of the war. Even now, more than two centuries later, it seems remarkable. His reason for taking the risk — and it was a huge risk —was his conviction that the depressed public spirit required some such stroke and, indeed, that the cause might not survive the winter without it. He ordered Lieutenant Colonel John Cadwalader with about 1,900 men to cross downstream of Trenton near Bristol (4) and engage the Hessian garrison of General Carl von Donop at Bordentown (5) as a diversion. Brigadier General James Ewing and 700 men were to cross directly opposite the town at Trenton Ferry (inset 6) and hold the bridge over the Assunpink River (inset 7) to seal off the Hessian escape from Trenton. Finally Washington himself would lead the main body of 2,400 men across the Delaware at McKonkey's Ferry (8) nine miles upstream from Trenton and advance on the city from the north. Virtually the entire army was to be employed in the attack.

Things began to go wrong immediately. Though Washington did not know of it, both Ewing and Cadwalader failed to carry out their parts of the plan. Ewing simply decided that the river was too angry to attempt a crossing. Cadwalader successfully transported the bulk of his militia across the river, but could not get his artillery across. Since he was reluctant to engage the enemy without it, he re-crossed the river to the Pennsylvania side, and was in the midst of writing an explanatory letter to Washington when he heard the sound of firing from Trenton.

Washington's men did cross the river, artillery and all. Though they were several hours behind schedule and the winter rain made the soldier's powder uncertain, Washington grimly ordered them to push on. His men advanced in two columns: Greene commanded the left which advanced along the Pennington Road, and Sullivan commanded the right which followed the River road. Both columns reached the outskirts of the city at a few minutes before eight in the morning.

The 1,400 Hessians at Trenton were commanded by Colonel Johann Gottlieb Rall who had led the Hessian attack on Chatterton's Hill at White Plains. Though tradition has it that the Americans caught the Germans sleeping off hangovers, Rall had in fact placed pickets on the main roads and these pickets brought news of the American advance in time for Rall to muster his regiments. Nevertheless, the Americans had superior numbers and the initiative, and Colonel Henry Knox's artillery at the head of King and Queen Streets (inset, 9) dominated the town. Rall attempted to drive off the Americans with a bayonet charge up King Street, but Knox's guns, and the men of General Hugh Mercer's brigade firing into his left flank, drove him back. Rall withdrew to an orchard southeast of town and attempted to rally, but he fell mortally wounded. His men discovered that they were virtually surrounded and they capitulated. The Americans lost only four killed and eight wounded in the battle while the Hessians lost 22 killed and 918 captured. About 500 escaped over the Assunpink toward Bordentown.

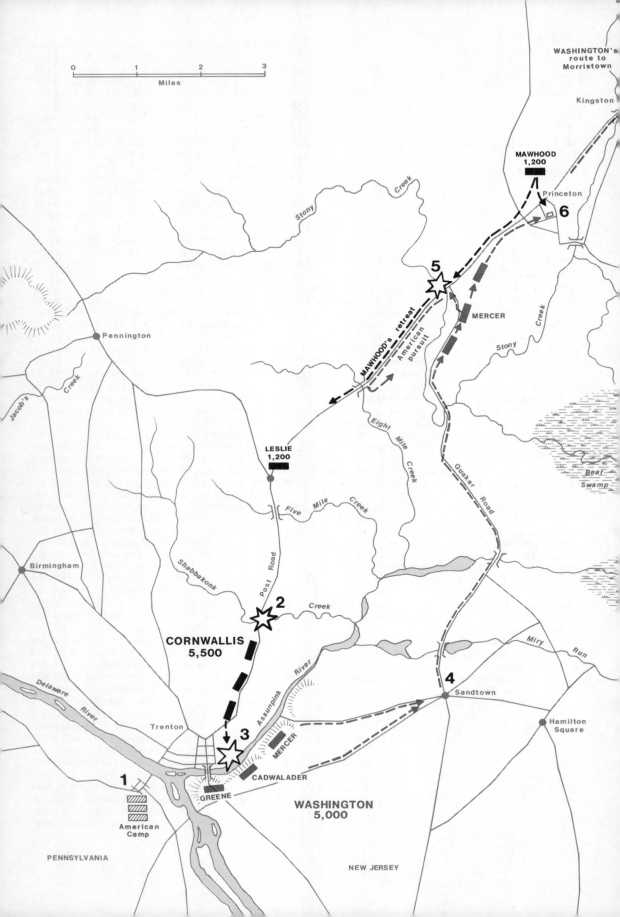

WASHINGTON's
route to
Morristown

Kingston

0   1   2   3
Miles

MAWHOOD
1,200

Stony   Creek

Princeton

6

5

MAWHOOD's retreat

American pursuit

MERCER

Stony   Creek

Pennington

LESLIE
1,200

Eight   Mile   Creek

Quaker   Road

Bear
Swamp

Five   Mile   Creek

Jacob's   Creek

Birmingham

Shabbakonk

Post Road

2

CORNWALLIS
5,500

Creek

Miry   Run

4

Sandtown

Hamilton
Square

Assunpink   River

Trenton

3

MERCER

Delaware   River

CADWALADER

1

GREENE

American
Camp

WASHINGTON
5,000

PENNSYLVANIA

NEW JERSEY

MAP # 11

Princeton

January 2, 1777

Washington hoped to follow up a victory at Trenton by heading toward the next British outpost at Princeton. But without Cadwalader's and Ewing's men at hand, he decided instead to recross the Delaware and return to his camp on the Pennsylvania side of the river (1). In so doing he under-estimated the impact of his victory on von Donop, who abandoned the line of the Delaware River, withdrew Hessian troops from Bordentown, and fell back to Allentown (off the map to the east). On the day after the battle, Cadwalader crossed into New Jersey and reported that there was no enemy in sight. As a result, Washington crossed the river again on December 30 and sent forces ahead to Five Mile Run to guard the Post Road to Princeton.

But Trenton prompted Howe into activity as well. The British commander cancelled Cornwallis's planned leave and ordered him into New Jersey with 8,000 men to deal with the brash Washington. As the Americans stepped out on the road to Princeton, Cornwallis was charging southward from New York determined to destroy the American army and end the rebellion once and for all.

Cornwallis left a rear guard of 1,200 men under Lieutenant Colonel Charles Mawhood at Princeton, and another 1,200 under General Alexander Leslie at Maidenhead (now Lawrenceville) and continued on toward Trenton with 5,500. Heavy rains made the roads difficult and American skirmishers disputed his advance especially at Shabbakonk Creek two miles north of Trenton (2). Nevertheless, the advance elements of his forces entered Trenton on January 1 to find the Americans dug in on a low ridge of hills behind Assinpunk Creek (3).

Cornwallis arrived in the late afternoon and looked over the American position. Rather than order an attack in the growing darkness, he decided to wait until the morning. Sir William Erskine, Cornwallis's quartermaster general, warned him that Washington probably would not be there in the morning, but Cornwallis was skeptical. Washington had no line of retreat; his back was to the river. Where, Cornwallis asked rhetorically, could he go?

Where indeed? Once again Washington came up with a plan of operations that was born of desperation. He left 400 men behind to keep the campfires burning and to make digging and entrenching sounds, and led the rest off in a night march, not southward, but east toward Sandtown (4) and then via the Quaker Road northward towards Princeton. As the sun came up on January 2, the American army was crossing Stony Creek only two miles from Princeton. At Stony Creek Washington detached General Hugh Mercer's brigade of 350 men to secure the Post Road to Trenton, both to prevent a British escape from the trap he was about to spring, and to warn of any British advance from Trenton.

But Mawhood, as it turned out, was already on the road to Trenton. He had left early that morning with 800 men to join Cornwallis at Trenton. Mawhood spied Mercer's brigade emerging from the woods and immediately attacked (5). The two sides exchanged volleys, but the Americans were weary from so much marching and fighting in the past week and they could not stand up to a British bayonet charge. They broke and fled. Cadwalader's Pennsylvania militia, coming to their support, fared no better. Only when Washington himself appeared on the scene did the Americans rally. Colonel Daniel Hitchcock's brigade of Continentals arrived and steadied the American line. Washington assumed personal command and led them to the attack. "Parade with us, my brave fellows," he called out to those headed for the rear. "There is but a handful of the enemy, and we will have them directly!" Other American forces, marching to the sound of the guns, closed in on Mawhood's flanks. The British were nearly surrounded and they began to fall back. Recognizing that he had bitten off more than he could chew, Mawhood ordered another bayonet charge to achieve a breakout to the south and his forces fled southward toward Trenton. The jubilant Americans pursued them for several miles and rounded up fifty prisoners, but Washington called off the pursuit to turn his attention to the British regiment that Mawhood had left behind in Princeton. Most of that now-orphaned regiment escaped to New Brunswick, but nearly 200 barricaded themselves in Nassau Hall (6). They hoped, perhaps, that its thick walls would deter the Americans from an assault. Captain Alexander Hamilton brought up an artillery piece, fired two rounds into the building, and ordered a charge. The British capitulated.

Washington had achieved another improbable victory. The Americans had suffered 23 killed, among them the promising General Mercer, and 20 wounded. The British lost 28 killed, 58 wounded, and 323 captured. Washington was eager to continue up the chain of British outposts to New Brunswick, but the condition of his elated but exhausted men convinced him that he had pushed his luck about as far as it would go. He headed instead for his winter campsite in Morristown. This time the campaigning season for the year really was over.

PART TWO

1777: The Turning Point

The winter of 1776-77 was a hard one for those of Washington's soldiers who endured it at Morristown. Though a hundred patriotic speeches a year refer to the trials of Valley Forge where many of these same men spent the winter of 1777-78, the conditions at Morristown were hardly better. Certainly they suffered more than did Howe's men, quartered in New York City. In addition to their physical discomfort, the Americans had the knowledge that except for the small but exhilerating victories at Trenton and Princeton, they had met everywhere with failure. The city of New York was in enemy hands and Howe's veteran professionals had bested them at every turn.

In addition there was bitter feuding within the American officer corps. Officers from New York continued to distrust officers from New England. Benedict Arnold and Ethan Allen personified this distrust. The two had collaborated grudgingly in the seizure of Ticonderoga in 1775, and Washington had found it necessary to give Arnold an independent command during the invasion of Canada in 1776. As the campaign season of 1777 opened, the rift widened. Major General Arthur St. Clair, the American commander at Fort Ticonderoga was the target of ridiculous but vicious rumors of disloyalty. Indeed, the distrust of St. Clair was so strong as to spawn absurd stories that he was in the pay of the British army. After the fall of Ticonderoga (see MAP # 13), popular opinion had it that St. Clair had evacuated the fort because a British sharpshooter had fired silver bullets into the fort as payment for an American withdrawal. The commander of the northern

John Burgoyne surrenders his sword to Horatio Gates at Saratoga in this painting by John Trumbull. Major General John Phillips stands behind Burgoyne and Daniel Morgan, who played an important role in the battle, stands to Gates' left dressed in homespun. Burgoyne's capitulation was decisive in bringing about an American alliance with France and therefore marked the turning point of the war. (NA)

army, Major General Philip Schuyler, was also the target of jealousy and suspicion. As a New Yorker descended from the original Dutch settlers, Schuyler was distrusted by New England officers. Responding to their criticism, none of it justified, Congress replaced Schuyler with Horatio Gates in August, just prior to the climactic battle of the campaign.

John Adams called 1777 "the year of the hangman" because the numeral contained the representation of three gallows. This lugubrious description notwithstanding, that year witnessed the turning point of the war. The decisive campaign was the defeat of British Major General John Burgoyne in New York and the first seven maps in the following section are devoted to that campaign (see MAPS # 12-18). The four remaining maps (# 19-22) are devoted to the campaign of Sir William Howe against Philadelphia which was also important in restoring American morale. Though Howe succeeded in capturing the American capital city, Washington's army performed creditably, and gave promise of future excellence. By the end of 1777, the British controlled only Newport, New York City, and Philadelphia.

The destruction of Burgoyne's army at Saratoga was the key event of 1777 and was nothing short of disastrous for the British. The illegitimate son of Lord Bingley, Major General John Burgoyne owed his rise to prominence to a spectacular marriage to Lady Charlotte Stanley, daughter of the Earl of Derby. At first repudiated by her family, Burgoyne was eventually accepted and the family influence was instrumental in gaining him preferment and promotion. During the waning months of the Seven Years War, Burgoyne served with distinction as a cavalry officer in Portugal where one of his subordinate officers had been Charles Lee. Yet somehow, despite his preferment at court and his success in the field, Burgoyne was never fully accepted by the British aristocracy in which he moved; there was the fact of his birth, and there were persistent rumors that his luck at card games was a product of Burgoyne's tendency to target intoxicated gentlemen of wealth as his card partners, a practice akin to cheating in the minds of many. Inclined to high living, he was an unlikely candidate for a wilderness campaign, yet that is exactly what he proposed.

As early as the summer of 1775, Burgoyne wrote from Boston to suggest a grand campaign to divide and conquer the American colonies. He proposed: "A large army of such foreign troops as might be hired to begin their operations up the Hudson River [from New York]; another army composed partly of old disciplined troops and partly of Canadians, to act from Canada; a large levy of Indians, and a supply of arms for the blacks, to awe the southern provinces, conjointly with detachments of regulars; and a numerous fleet to sweep the whole coast, might possibly do the business in one campaign."

In essence, this outline became the basis for Burgoyne's 1777 campaign. When Carleton retired to St. Johns after the Battle of Valcour Island in the fall of 1776 (see MAP # 7), Burgoyne had opposed the decision. He did not complain directly to Carleton, but instead expressed his disapproval in letters to influential friends in England. Moreover, he took those opinions back with him to London during his winter leave. There Burgoyne offered a document entitled "Thoughts for Conducting the War From the Side of Canada," a detailed proposal for an offensive in the spring along the Lake Champlain - Lake George route to Albany. His suggestion had a ready audience at court. By the spring his proposals had not only been accepted as policy, but he had received a commission to supersede Carleton in command of the northern army and put them into execution.

If Burgoyne should be credited with originating the scheme, he is also largely responsible for its failure. Despite his recent experience with Carleton's army, he seems to have underestimated the increased "friction" of operating in a virtual wilderness. Particularly after the fall of Fort Ticonderoga, his conduct of the campaign was marred by poor decision-making, hesitancy, and finally a lack of will. To him must go a large share of the responsibility for the British loss of the American colonies, for intelligence of Burgoyne's defeat was the catalyst that led France to recognize the independence of the United States and to sign an alliance that dramatically changed the balance of power in the conflict, especially sea power. Without a doubt it was the turning point of the war.

Major General John Burgoyne had excellent connections at court. He was married to the daughter of the Earl of Derby and was himself a member of the House of Commons though he was not often in attendance. Moreover, he moved in that level of society where important political and military decisions were made. He was also an amateur poet and playwright as well as a frequent and successful card player and sportsman. (NA)

Major General Horatio Gates replaced Philip Schuyler in command of the American Northern Army just prior to the Battles of Freeman's Farm and Bemis Heights (see MAPS #16 & 18). After the American victory, he bypassed Washington and reported directly to Congress, an act that may have been motivated by an ambition to be promoted to the top command position. (NA)

Major General Benedict Arnold was without a doubt the most important figure in the American army during the Saratoga campaign. His dramatic leadership at Freeman's Farm and Bemis Heights secured the American victory. If the bullet that wounded him at Bemis Heights had been fatal, he might today be one of America's most revered heroes. (NA)

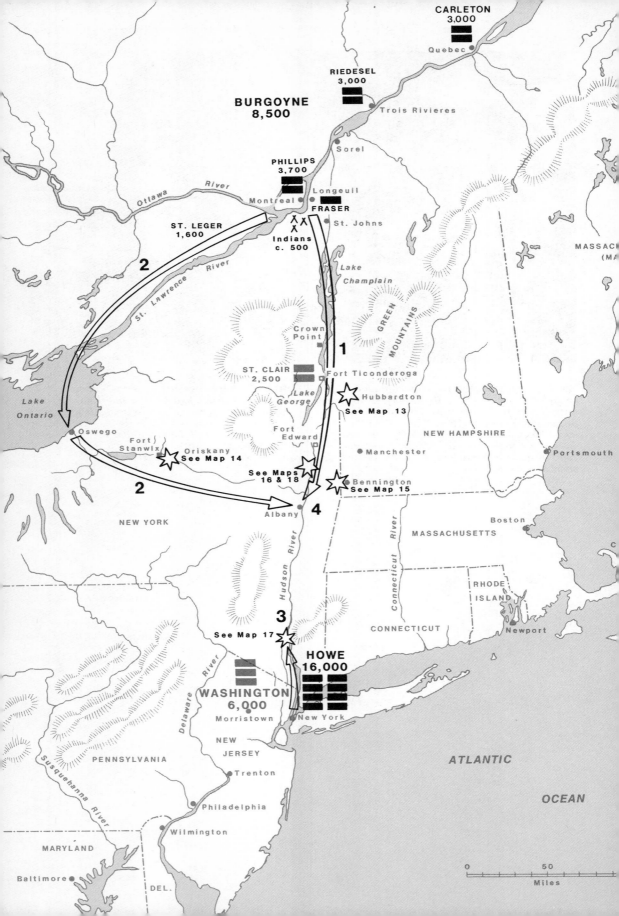

CARLETON
3,000

Quebec

RIEDESEL
3,000

Trois Rivieres

BURGOYNE
8,500

Sorel

PHILLIPS
3,700

Longueuil

Montreal

FRASER

St. Johns

St. Leger
1,600

Ottawa River

Indians
c. 500

2

St. Lawrence River

Lake
Champlain

GREEN
MOUNTAINS

Crown
Point

1

Lake
Ontario

ST. CLAIR
2,500

Fort Ticonderoga

MASSACHUSETTS
(MA

Oswego

Fort
Stanwix

Lake
George

Hubbardton

See Map 13

NEW HAMPSHIRE

Oriskany
See Map 14

Fort
Edward

Manchester

Portsmouth

2

See Maps
16 & 18

Bennington
See Map 15

4

Albany

Boston

NEW YORK

MASSACHUSETTS

Connecticut River

Hudson River

RHODE
ISLAND

CONNECTICUT

Newport

3

See Map 17

HOWE
16,000

WASHINGTON
6,000

Morristown

New York

ATLANTIC

Delaware River

NEW
JERSEY

Trenton

OCEAN

Susquehanna River

PENNSYLVANIA

Philadelphia

Wilmington

MARYLAND

0   50

DEL.

Miles

Baltimore

MAP # 12

Burgoyne's Plan

Spring, 1777

Burgoyne's plan for the conquest of America was not unusual or even particularly original. It was based on the assumption that New England was the center of disaffection in America and that if it could be separated from the rest of the colonies, the rebellion could be limited and eventually defeated. The central element of the plan was an advance southward from Canada along the Lake Champlain-Lake George waterway (1). Such a route was ordained by the geography of the region; any campaign on the Canadian frontier had to depend on the waterways because of the absence of any roads. Both sides had relied on this historic route during the Seven Years War and had built forts along it as barriers to the enemy and as springboards for invasions of their own.

A second element of Burgoyne's plan was for a smaller detachment of 800 British and Canadians under Colonel Barry St. Leger, with an equal number of Indian allies, to move up the St. Lawrence River to Lake Ontario and from there to proceed down the Mohawk River Valley (2). The objective of this offensive was to demonstrate British strength in the Mohawk Valley in order to impress the chiefs of the powerful Iroquois nation. In addition, the British believed that the large number of loyalists in the area would take a more active role in the war with the appearance of British troops.

As a third element, Burgoyne's plan also called for Howe's forces at New York to move northward up the Hudson River (3) to engage American forces that might otherwise be sent against Burgoyne. The plan did not presume that it would be necessary for Howe to advance all the way to Albany, but anticipated that he would make a diversion in that direction. Confronted by these three simultaneous offensives, the Americans would be unable to concentrate against any one of them.

The two northern prongs of this triple offensive would meet at Albany (4), the only inland American city of any consequence.

Most historians have been critical of Burgoyne's plan. They point out that the three elements of the operation were too far apart to be mutually supporting. Instead of putting the American forces in a position where they were being attacked simultaneously from three sides, the plan allowed the Americans to concentrate their forces against each element of the British offensive separately. In addition, the coordination of military forces across such a large area was virtually impossible. Once Burgoyne set off on his campaign, communication with the commanders of the other columns would be all but impossible. Finally, Burgoyne's plan called for the involvement of Howe's army at New York, but Howe's exact responsibilities were never clearly outlined by Burgoyne or by anyone else. Howe after all was Burgoyne's senior in rank and any orders to him would therefore have to come from the Colonial Secretary Lord George Germain. But Germain was an ocean away and when he did send orders to Howe, they were vague and discretionary.

Burgoyne arrived at Montreal on May 6, 1777 and held a grand review of his forces. The army was somewhat the worse for wear after a Canadian winter. The long tails of their scarlet coats had been cut off and the material used to patch what were now short jackets, and the men had cut the brims off of their elaborate hats turning them into trim little caps. But their morale was good and they had clear superiority of numbers. The four thousand troops at Montreal were under the direct command of Major General William Phillips, while the British advance guard at Longeuil, composed of the light infantry and grenadier companies, was under the command of Brigadier General Simon Fraser. The 3,000 German mercenaries at Trois Rivières were under the command of Major General Baron von Riedesel, and the German advance guard, composed of Brunswick dragoons, was commanded by Lieutenant Colonel Heinrich Breyman. Particularly unsuited for frontier combat, the German dragoons wore huge jack boots that weighed twelve pounds each, leather gauntlets, and giant plumed hats. In addition to these forces, Burgoyne also attracted a large number of Indians for his campaign — perhaps a thousand or more — but management of his Indian allies would become one of his most serious problems and prove to be at least as much a liability as an asset.

Unlike the previous year, when Carleton had to contend with Benedict Arnold's little fleet before committing his army to the lake, this time the British held undisputed command of the waterway, for the Americans had not rebuilt their fleet. On June 13, Burgoyne stepped aboard his pinnace at St. Johns and the expedition got underway. Hundreds of watercraft, from ship-rigged vessels to the darting canoes of the Indians, headed southward up the lake toward the first major obstacle in Burgoyne's path: the American fort at Ticonderoga.

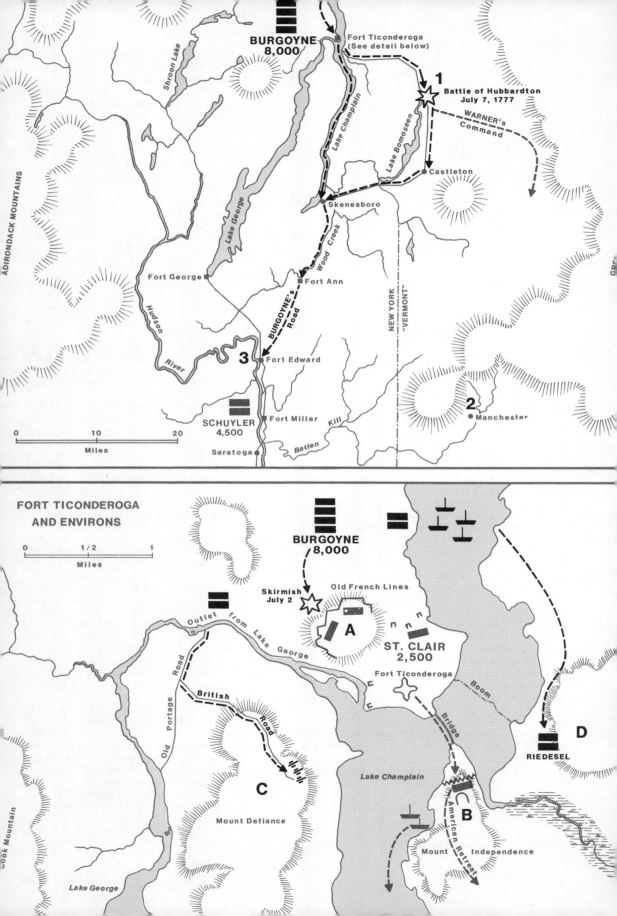

BURGOYNE
8,000

Fort Ticonderoga
(See detail below)

1 Battle of Hubbardton
July 7, 1777

WARNER's
Command

Castleton

Skenesboro

Fort George

Fort Ann

BURGOYNE's Road

3 Fort Edward

SCHUYLER
4,500

Fort Miller

2 Manchester

Saratoga

0   10   20
Miles

ADIRONDACK MOUNTAINS

Shroon Lake

Lake Champlain

Lake Bomoseen

Lake George

Hudson River

Wood Creek

NEW YORK "VERMONT"

Batten Kill

FORT TICONDEROGA
AND ENVIRONS

0   1/2   1
Miles

BURGOYNE
8,000

Skirmish
July 2

Old French Lines

A

ST. CLAIR
2,500

Fort Ticonderoga

Outlet from Lake George

Old Portage Road

British Road

C

Mount Defiance

Lake Champlain

Boom

Bridge

American Retreat

B

D

RIEDESEL

Mount Independence

Lake George

Cook Mountain

MAP # 13

Ticonderoga and Hubbardton

July 5-7, 1777

Of all the fortifications built along the historic Lake Champlain-Lake George invasion route, the most important and the most imposing was Fort Ticonderoga. Built by the French in 1755 and named Fort Carillon after the musical noise of the falls that spilled over the outlet from Lake George into Lake Champlain, it guarded the only feasible route south to the Hudson River. After the defeat of France in the Seven Years War, Ticonderoga was garrisoned by a small British caretaking force from which Ethan Allen and Benedict Arnold had seized it in May, 1775. Now, two years later, the American commander at Ticonderoga was Major General Arthur St. Clair who arrived on June 12, 1777, only one day before Burgoyne embarked in his pinnace at St. Johns.

St. Clair had 2,500 men to defend this vital position, far too few to meet Burgoyne in the open field, and too few even to man all the far-flung defenses of the fort. Strong as it was, Ticonderoga was surrounded by hills that, if occupied by an enemy, would render the fort helpless (see lower map). A mile to the north, within easy artillery range, were heights where the French Marquis de Montcalm had built earthworks to repel a British attack in 1758 (A). A mile in the opposite direction, across the lake narrows, was another height called Mount Independence by the Americans which also had to be manned (B). A third hill, the highest of them all, was a mile to the west (C). But the Americans ignored this mountain, appropriately named Mount Defiance, because it was beyond musket range and was inaccessible to artillery — or so it was believed. With his 2,500 men spread out in these far flung defenses, St. Clair's position was extremely precarious.

Screened by their Indian allies, the British advanced up Lake Champlain at a leisurely pace. On July 1, they landed a few miles north of Ticonderoga; the British were on the western bank, the Germans on the east. The British approached the main American defense positions along the old French lines with caution. At about three in the

afternoon on July 2 the advanced elements of Fraser's light infantry began sniping at the American position and provoked a furious series of volleys, though when the smoke cleared no one had been injured on either side. Riedesel pushed forward to the marshy banks of Eagle Creek at the foot of Mount Independence (D) where his men came under fire from American batteries on the heights.

Assessing the situation, Burgoyne saw immediately that Mount Defiance commanded all of the American works including the fort, and the water route south as well. He sent a team to its summit to ascertain the practicability of dragging field guns to its crest. The report was enthusiastic and General Phillips remarked: "Where a goat can go, a man can go; and where a man can go, he can drag a gun." On July 5, British artillerists and engineers began cutting a road up the reverse slope of Mount Defiance. Burgoyne hoped to spring a surprise on the Americans and force their unconditional capitulation, but the Americans spied British artillery officers near the crest of the mountain and St. Clair immediately called a council of his officers. Their unanimous decision was to evacuate the fort and escape southward while they still could. They abandoned the fort that night, 400 of them by water up the extension of Lake Champlain to Skenesboro, and the rest across the floating bridge to Mount Independence and then along the road to Hubbardton and Castleton (see upper map).

The next morning the British discovered that their quarry had flown the coop. Fraser's light infantry and grenadiers set off in pursuit followed by von Riedesel's Germans. Fraser's 750 men caught up with the American rear guard under Colonel Seth Warner just north of Hubbardton (1). The Americans had a total of three regiments, about the same number of men as Fraser, but they were completely unaware that the British were so close. Colonel Nathan Hale's New Hampshire regiment was surprised at breakfast and overrun; the other two American regiments recovered from their initial surprise and fought forest-style from behind trees. Fraser directed a flanking column to the right behind the Americans to cut them off from their road to Castleton. The appearance of von Riedesel's Germans made Warner realize that his force was in danger of annihilation. He shouted to his men to scatter and meet later at Manchester (2) and the Americans fled in small groups into the forest.

Burgoyne had cracked the Ticonderoga hinge, in fact, had burst through the door. The few American units that escaped intact fell back all the way to Fort Edward on the Hudson (3). The route to Lake George lay open. But having advanced as far as Skenesboro, Burgoyne decided to ignore Lake George and advance to the Hudson via Wood Creek and Fort Ann. It was a fatal decision. Beyond Fort Ann Burgoyne's men would have to cut their own road through the wilderness, harassed at every opportunity by American scouting parties. It would take the British nearly a month to reach Fort Edward.

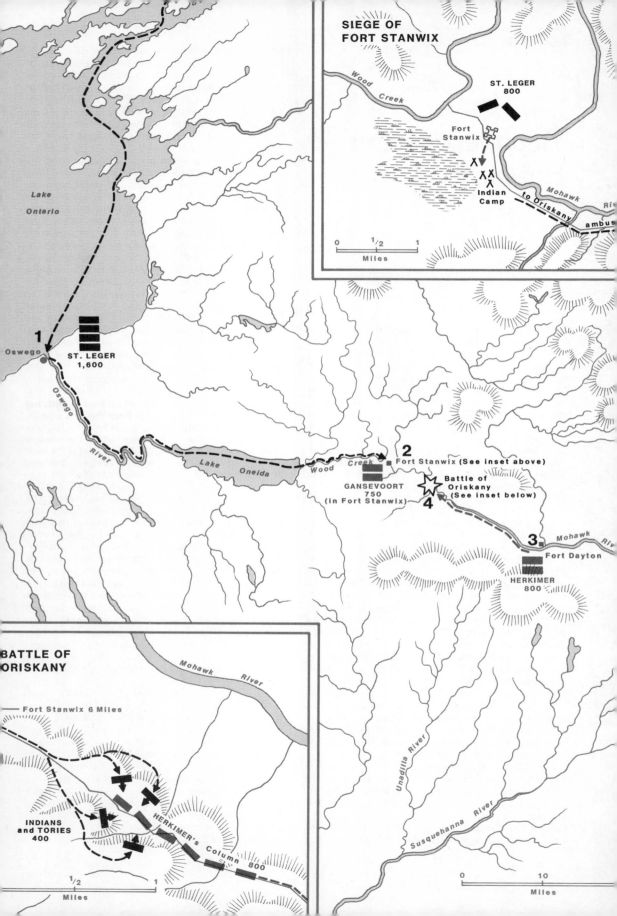

SIEGE OF FORT STANWIX

Wood Creek

ST. LEGER
800

Fort
Stanwix

Indian
Camp

to Oriskany

Mohawk
River

ambush

0   1/2   1
Miles

Lake
Ontario

Oswego

1

ST. LEGER
1,600

Oswego River

Lake Oneida

Wood Creek

2 Fort Stanwix (See inset above)

GANSEVOORT
750
(in Fort Stanwix)

4

Battle of
Oriskany
(See inset below)

3 Mohawk River
Fort Dayton

HERKIMER
800

Unadilla River

Susquehanna River

0   10
Miles

BATTLE OF
ORISKANY

Mohawk River

Fort Stanwix 6 Miles

INDIANS
and TORIES
400

HERKIMER's Column 800

1/2   1
Miles

MAP # 14

Fort Stanwix and Oriskany

August 1777

While Burgoyne's soldiers marched from Fort Ann to the Hudson, the second element of the British triple offensive began in western New York. With a force of some 800 British soldiers and Canadian volunteers and an equal number of Indian allies, Colonel Barry St. Leger traveled up the St. Lawrence from Montreal to Lake Ontario and disembarked at Fort Oswego (1) on July 25. The next day he started his forces up the Oswego River en route to the Mohawk Valley via Oneida Lake and Wood Creek.

The only military barrier in St. Leger's path was Fort Stanwix (2) at the site of present-day Rome, New York. Like Fort Ticonderoga, Stanwix had been built during the Seven Years War to guard a vital point in a major water route, in this case the portage between Wood Creek and the eastward-flowing Mohawk River. St. Leger had been told that the fort was all but abandoned, but in fact it was manned by 550 Continentals under the command of twenty-eight-year-old Colonel Peter Gansevoort.

St. Leger's advance guard arrived at Fort Stanwix on August 2 and missed by a single day intercepting a party of two hundred American reinforcements bringing supplies to the fort. The reinforcements brought Gansevoort's garrison up to 750 — nearly as many soldiers as there were in St. Leger's small army — and they brought food and supplies sufficient for six weeks. On August 3 St. Leger held a formal military review within sight of the fort's defenders and afterward sent Gansevoort a formal request to surrender, a request which the American refused. Since St. Leger's small field pieces made no impression on the walls of the fort (his largest gun was a four pounder) the British and their Indian allies settled in for a siege.

Upon hearing news of the British "invasion," Colonel Nicolas Herkimer, commander of the Tryon County militia, ordered out all men between 16 and 60 and managed to assemble some 800 militiamen at Fort Dayton (3), near the pres-

ent town of Herkimer, thirty miles down river from Stanwix. This column of citizen-soldiers left Fort Dayton on August 4 (encumbered by 400 ox carts), and camped about ten miles east of Fort Stanwix (4) on the night of August 5. When St. Leger learned of the proximity of Herkimer's relief column, most of his soldiers were off attempting to clear the obstructions from Wood Creek to open communications back to Fort Oswego. The British commander therefore sent about 400 Indians under Chief Joseph Brandt and a few Tories off to set an ambush for Herkimer's column.

The ambush was sprung at ten the next morning about six miles from the fort in a deep ravine that cut across the road (see lower inset). Despite a screen of friendly Oneida Indians acting as scouts, Herkimer's militiamen marched straight into the trap. Attacked simultaneously from all sides, the Americans formed themselves into a circle and fought back. Little quarter was asked or offered by either side and the fight was vigorous until rain showers slowed the action at about eleven. When the skies cleared, the tide of battle turned in favor of the militiamen. The Indians began to withdraw, and the Tories had no choice but to go with them. Casualties were heavy: the Americans lost 150 to 200 killed, 50 or so wounded, and some 200 captured. The Indians lost perhaps 150 killed. Meanwhile back at Fort Stanwix, Colonel Gansevoort had ordered Lieutenant Colonel Marius Willett, his second in command, to sortie from the fort and attack the camp of the besiegers. When the Indians who had survived the battle with Herkimer's militia returned, they discovered that Willett's men had seized or destroyed virtually all their personal possessions and camp equipment.

Both sides claimed victory in the Battle of Oriskany, as the ambush of Herkimer's column came to be known. The relief column turned back, but Willet's raid on the Indian encampment led to a great deal of unhappiness among St. Leger's Indian allies who had borne the brunt of the fighting. Somewhat desperate now, St. Leger threatened Gansevoort that unless he surrendered promptly, the British would not be able to guarantee that the Indians would not massacre the survivors. Gansevoort scornfully rejected all such proposals, but he also decided to send Willett out for reinforcements. At Fort Dayton, Willett met Benedict Arnold coming to the fort's relief with 900 Continentals.

The decision to send Arnold to Fort Stanwix with a relief column was made by Philip Schuyler who commanded the main American army at Stillwater on the Hudson. It was a risky decision. Schuyler had only 4,500 men, and Burgoyne, who arrived at Fort Edward only twenty five miles to the north on July 29, had nearly twice as many. All of Schuyler's officers except Benedict Arnold had opposed the decision. But Schuyler's decision proved wise, for news of Arnold's mission and exaggerated accounts of his numbers spread by American spies, convinced St. Leger's disgruntled Indian allies to decamp. Abandoned by his Indians, St. Leger had no choice but to raise the siege and retreat the way he had come.

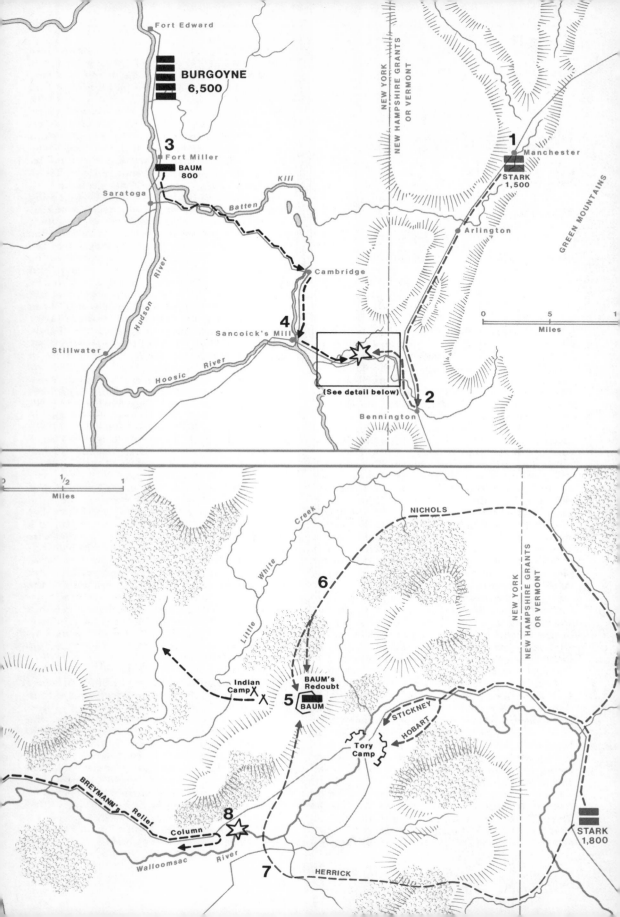

Fort Edward

BURGOYNE
6,500

3 Fort Miller
BAUM
800

Saratoga

Batten Kill

Hudson River

Stillwater

Sancoick's Mill

Hoosic River

4

Cambridge

1 Manchester
STARK
1,500

Arlington

NEW YORK
NEW HAMPSHIRE GRANTS OR VERMONT

GREEN MOUNTAINS

0   5   1
Miles

(See detail below)

2

Bennington

---

0   1/2   1
Miles

White Creek

Little Creek

NICHOLS

6

Indian Camp

5 BAUM's
Redoubt
BAUM

STICKNEY

HOBART

Tory Camp

NEW YORK
NEW HAMPSHIRE GRANTS OR VERMONT

STARK
1,800

BREYMANN'S Relief Column

Walloomsac River

8

7 HERRICK

MAP # 15

Bennington

August 16, 1777

Having spent nearly a month cutting a road from Fort Ann to the Hudson River, Burgoyne's soldiers were happy to leave the wilderness behind. None were happier than the Brunswick dragoons under Lieutenant Colonel Friedrich Baum. Clubbing along in their giant boots and dragging their useless sabres, they were eager to find mounts for themselves and enter Albany in a style proper for cavalry. Burgoyne was willing, but the Americans had stripped the nearby countryside of all usable military stores, including horses and cattle. Baum suggested that his men be allowed to forage for horses off to the east in the rich and fertile Connecticut Valley. Burgoyne agreed, though he later modified Baum's orders limiting his expedition to the area around the village of Bennington where the rebels reportedly had established an arms cache. Baum's column of some 800 men contained about 300 German dragoons, an equal number of Tories, a handful of British light infantry, and a hundred or so Indians to act as scouts.

The target of Baum's foraging mission was the New Hampshire Grants, an area over which Americans had squabbled for decades. Burgoyne had been informed that the area was lightly defended, but his information was out of date. Colonel John Stark, a New Hampshire native who had distinguished himself in the Continental army but had resigned in disgust when Congress failed to promote him, had gathered a small army of some 1,500 men in the Connecticut River Valley. In the first week of August Stark moved his men to Manchester (1) where the remnants of Seth Warner's command had rendezvoused after their drubbing at Hubbardton, and on August 8, he marched them twenty miles south to Bennington (2).

Baum's column set out from Fort Miller (3) on August 11. It first encountered opposition from American skirmishers at Sancoick's Mill (4) where about 200 men in fringed hunting shirts fired a volley from cover and then withdrew. The next day, August 14, Baum entered the beautiful Walloomsac River Valley (see lower map) where

Stark's small army waited four miles northwest of Bennington. Both forces went into bivouac to assess the situation. On the fifteenth a heavy rain kept both armies in place, but recognizing that he was outnumbered, Baum sent for reinforcements and dug in. He established his headquarters atop a rounded hill overlooking the valley and ordered his men to build a breastwork (5). The small fort would not accommodate all of Baum's command; the Tories and light infantry dug in near the road where it crossed the river.

On August 16 the Americans attacked. Considering the inexperience of his men and the roughness of the terrain, Stark's plan was a complicated one. He decided on nothing less than a double envelopment. Colonel Moses Nichols was to lead some 300 men around the shoulder of a nearby mountain and attack Baum's redoubt from the north (6) while Colonel Samuel Herrick with another 300 attacked from the south and west (7). Smaller groups under Colonels Thomas Stickney and David Hobart were to assault the camps of the Tories and the light infantry. When the flanking attacks were well launched, Stark would lead the main body, nearly 1,200 men, in a frontal assault. Incredibly, the attack worked exactly as planned. When Baum first spotted Nichols' men approaching from the west, he believed they were friendly Tories coming to his aid. Only when the Americans opened fire at close range, did Baum appreciate their true character. Stark heard the sound of the firing and he called out to this men: "There they are! We'll beat them before night, or Molly Stark will be a widow!" as he led them to the attack.

The outlying units were overrun immediately; the Indians and Tories simply fled into the woods. Only Baum's redoubt manned by the German dragoons held firm. Baum's men held their attackers at bay until the dragoons ran out of ammunition. Even then, the Germans did not capitulate, but drew their sabres in an effort to fight their way out to the road. But when Baum fell mortally wounded, the spirit went out of the dragoons and they capitulated or fled into the forest.

Burgoyne, meanwhile, had dispatched Lieutenant Colonel Heinrich Breymann with 600 men as reinforcements. This force arrived in the valley of the Walloomsac too late to save Baum, but with Stark's forces completely disorganized after their triumph, Breyman threatened to snatch victory from defeat. Only the arrival of Seth Warner's 300 fresh troops from Manchester allowed Stark to launch a counter-attack. Another tough stand-up fight ensued (8). Like Baum, Breymann ordered a retreat only when his men were dangerously low on ammunition. During the retreat the Americans closed in and the retreat became a rout. At nightfall, the Americans called off their pursuit. The next day the German survivors staggered back into Burgoyne's camp. Altogether the expedition had cost Burgoyne almost a thousand men: 200 killed and 700 captured or missing; the American losses were 30 killed and 40 wounded. It was a stunning setback for Burgoyne and the first clear sign that his expedition was in serious trouble.

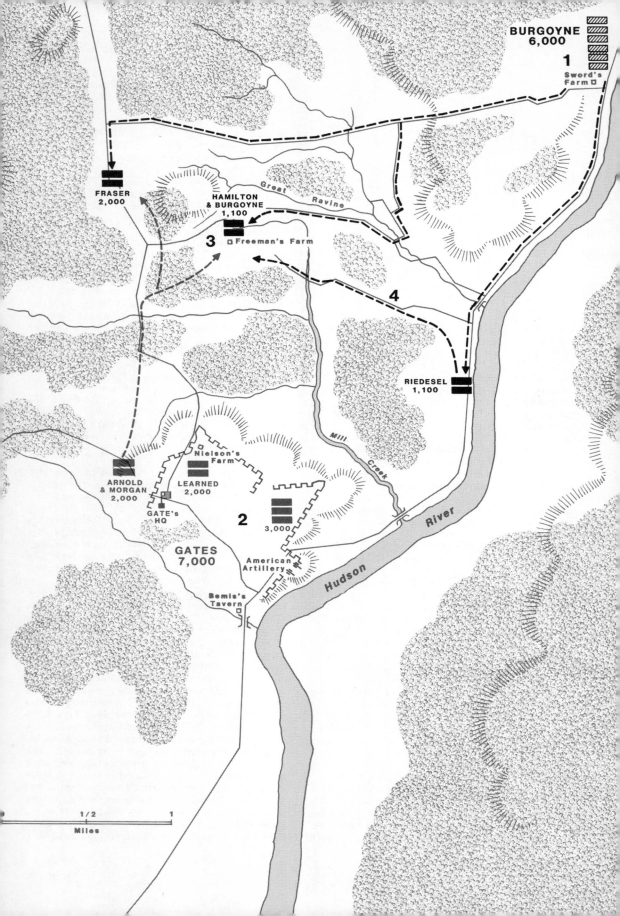

BURGOYNE
6,000

1

Sword's
Farm

FRASER
2,000

Great
Ravine

HAMILTON
& BURGOYNE
1,100

3

Freeman's Farm

4

RIEDESEL
1,100

Nielson's
Farm

Mill

ARNOLD
& MORGAN
2,000

LEARNED
2,000

GATE's
HQ

2

3,000

Creek

River

GATES
7,000

American
Artillery

Hudson

Bemis's
Tavern

1/2   1
Miles

MAP # 16

Freeman's Farm

September 19, 1777

Three days after Stark's victory at Bennington, Congress named Horatio Gates to supersede Philip Schuyler in command of the Northern Army in yet another episode of the feud between New England and New York officers. As luck would have it, Gates assumed command just at the moment when fortunes were turning in favor of the Americans. Hard on the heels of the news from Bennington came intelligence of St. Leger's retreat from western New York. In addition, tales of the gruesome activities of some of Burgoyne's Indian allies led more and more American volunteers to join Gates's army.

The most famous of the Indian atrocities was the murder of young Jane McCrea, the fiancée of a loyalist officer in Burgoyne's army. Apparently several of Burgoyne's Indian scouts argued over who would have the honor of escorting the woman into camp, and in the heat of the argument one of the Indians shot and scalped her and then carried his grisly trophy into camp where, as the story goes, it was recognized by her distraught lover. Though it was one incident among many in the history of frontier violence, this tale in particular touched the popular imagination. Gates referred to it in a letter of protest to Burgoyne — a letter which was re-printed throughout New England. The result was a spectacular increase in the number of American volunteers. With these new recruits, and the return of Arnold's men from Fort Stanwix, Gates soon commanded an army of 7,000 while Burgoyne's forces, after the losses at Bennington, shrunk to fewer than 6,000. In mid-August Burgoyne got more bad news. He learned that Howe's army at New York had sailed for the Delaware Bay on July 23. Burgoyne was on his own.

On September 13 and 14 Burgoyne's army crossed to the west bank of the Hudson River on a bridge of boats and began to march southward. Three days later it camped near Sword's Farm (1), four miles north of the American position on Bemis Heights.

Gates's position was a strong one. His army occupied a high bluff overlooking the Hudson River near Bemis's Tavern where the Polish engineer Colonel Thaddeus Kosciuszko had laid out strong entrenchments (2). On the right Gates placed the brigades of Glover, Nixon, and Patterson — about 3,000 men — and the bulk of his artillery. A little to the west, near a farmhouse belonging to a Mr. Nielson, Gates placed his center under Brigadier General Ebenezer Learned, and established his own headquarters. On his western or left flank, Gates placed Benedict Arnold with several New England regiments and the riflemen of Daniel Morgan. It was a strong position, but not unassailable. If the British could get around Arnold's flank, they could seize higher ground to the west and use their artillery to force the Americans out of their fortifications as they had at Fort Ticonderoga. For that reason, Arnold urged Gates to assail Burgoyne during his approach. But Gates rejected Arnold's advice and awaited a British attack.

During his confrontation with Gates's army, Burgoyne was literally groping in the dark. The area was so thickly wooded and the terrain so uneven, that Burgoyne had no clear picture of the American position. Nevertheless, at ten a.m. on September 19, Burgoyne began a tentative advance, sending his men forward in three divisions through the thick forest of mixed pine and hardwoods. Arnold begged Gates for permission to strike them and finally Gates agreed to send Morgan's riflemen forward and told Arnold that he could involve the rest of his command if the situation justified it. Around mid-day the center corps of Brigadier General John Hamilton, accompanied by Burgoyne himself, came under fire from the woods around the clearing at Freeman's Farm (3). Concentrating on the officers and the gunners, Morgan's men picked off the redcoats one by one until the frustrated British mounted a charge. Arnold brought his regiments forward and a general engagement ensued. The British forces were soon in serious trouble. Arnold sent word back to Gates that with a few reinforcements he could defeat the British altogether. But Gates not only refused to budge, he ordered Arnold back to the American lines, orders which Arnold ignored. For the British, the situation was saved by Riedesel who marched his men toward the sound of the guns and managed to drive off Arnold's impetuous attacks (4).

Riedesel's initiative prevented what might have turned into a full scale disaster for the British. Even as it was, though the British held the field at nightfall, they had suffered terrible casualties. Some 600 British, many of them officers, had fallen to the American marksmen while the Americans had suffered fewer than 300 casualties. In addition, the fighting spirit of many of Burgoyne's veterans had been shaken by the character of the wilderness battle. Moreover, they knew that Gates's army still lay across their intended line of advance.

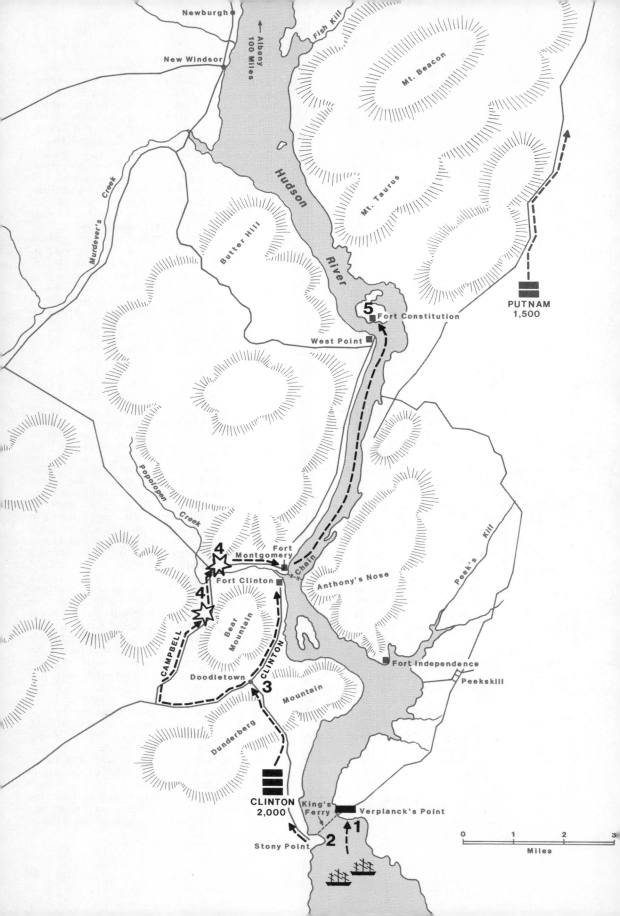

Newburgh

New Windsor

Albany
100 Miles

Murdever's Creek

Fish Kill

Hudson River

Mt. Beacon

Mt. Taurus

Butter Hill

5 Fort Constitution

West Point

PUTNAM
1,500

Popolopen Creek

4 Fort Montgomery

Chain

Fort Clinton

Anthony's Nose

Peek's Kill

4

CAMPBELL

Bear Mountain

CLINTON

Doodletown

3

Mountain

Fort Independence

Peekskill

Dunderberg

CLINTON
2,000

King's Ferry

Verplanck's Point

1

Stony Point

2

0   1   2   3

Miles

MAP # 17

The Highlands

October 6, 1777

Burgoyne had planned to renew his attack on the American position at Bemis Heights as soon as possible, but two days after the Battle of Freeman's Farm, he changed his mind. He received a message from Sir Henry Clinton, whom Howe had left in command at New York, in which Sir Henry offered to initiate a move up the Hudson River Valley to threaten the Americans from the south. Enthusiastically accepting Clinton's offer, Burgoyne decided to postpone a second attack of his own until he could determine what effect Clinton's maneuver might have on Gates.

Clinton was too undermanned to attempt a full scale offensive all the way to Albany —he had only 4,000 British troops and some 3,000 Tories to defend New York City —but he planned to make a demonstration against the American forts guarding the Highlands where the Hudson River narrows to a half mile wide some forty miles north of the city. Clinton received reinforcements from England on September 24 and he started northward with about 3,000 men on October 3.

The two American forts that were the target of Clinton's expedition were, ironically enough, also under the command of a Clinton: Major General (and Governor of New York) George Clinton. The American Clinton had only about 600 men under arms to defend Fort Clinton and Fort Montgomery. Major General Israel Putnam commanded a field army in the vicinity, but having responded in recent months to repeated pleas for reinforcements from both Washington and Gates, his forces were now reduced to some 1,500 men. Moreover, the British took Putnam's army out of the picture almost immediately by a simple strategem. Sir Henry landed about a thousand men on Verplanck's Point (1) on the east bank of the Hudson on October 5 and Putnam, assuming that he was the target of the British move, withdrew to the interior and called for reinforcements. The British were thus freed to concentrate on the two American forts on the western bank without fear of interference from Putnam.

Leaving a thousand men at Verplanck's Point, Sir Henry ordered the rest of the British army to cross the river and land at Stony Point (2). From there the British began a march around the shoulder of massive Dunderberg Mountain. The path was narrow and precipitous, tailor-made for an ambush, but the British encountered no Americans until they arrived at Doodletown (3). There Sir Henry divided his forces; he sent 900 men under Lieutenant Colonel Archibald Campbell to the east around the back of Bear Mountain to attack Fort Montgomery, and led the remaining 1,200 against Fort Clinton.

The American Clinton, meanwhile, was presiding over a meeting of the state legislature at Esophus (Kingston) in his capacity as governor, but he abandoned the conference and returned to the forts when he received news of the British attack. From the forts, he sent out two groups of 100 men each to operate against the advancing British columns. Colonel Campbell's men had to fight two sharp skirmishes (4) before they reached the outskirts of Fort Montgomery. The larger group under Sir Henry had little trouble until it reached the outer defenses of Fort Clinton in the late afternoon. The British sent in demands for surrender which the Americans rejected, and the redcoats thereupon mounted an assault. They took heavy losses from American musket fire, but in the end they overwhelmed the defenders and the Americans threw down their arms or fled into the forest. Governor Clinton, his brother James (who commanded Fort Montgomery), and about half of the American defenders escaped, but American losses numbered nearly 300 in all categories, plus the loss of 100 cannon in the forts, as compared to British losses of about 150.

The British rather easily cut their way through the barrier of chains and logs across the river and assaulted the squadron of American warships on the river which included two frigates. They captured one American schooner and the Americans set fire to the rest of their fleet to prevent its sharing the same fate. The next day Sir Henry Clinton sent a small force up to Fort Constitution (5), opposite West Point. Its garrison abandoned the fort and melted into the forest. The American barrier had collapsed, and more importantly the river was opened to navigation for another forty miles to the north. Clinton wrote Burgoyne that he hoped his success would "facilitate your operations." But Fort Constitution was still more than a hundred miles away from Gates's army and by the time Clinton got around to sending General John Vaughn upriver to Esophus, halfway to Albany, on October 22, Burgoyne's expedition had already reached a crisis. On the same day that British forces captured Fort Constitution, Burgoyne and Gates fought what proved to be a decisive engagement in front of the American lines on Bemis Heights.

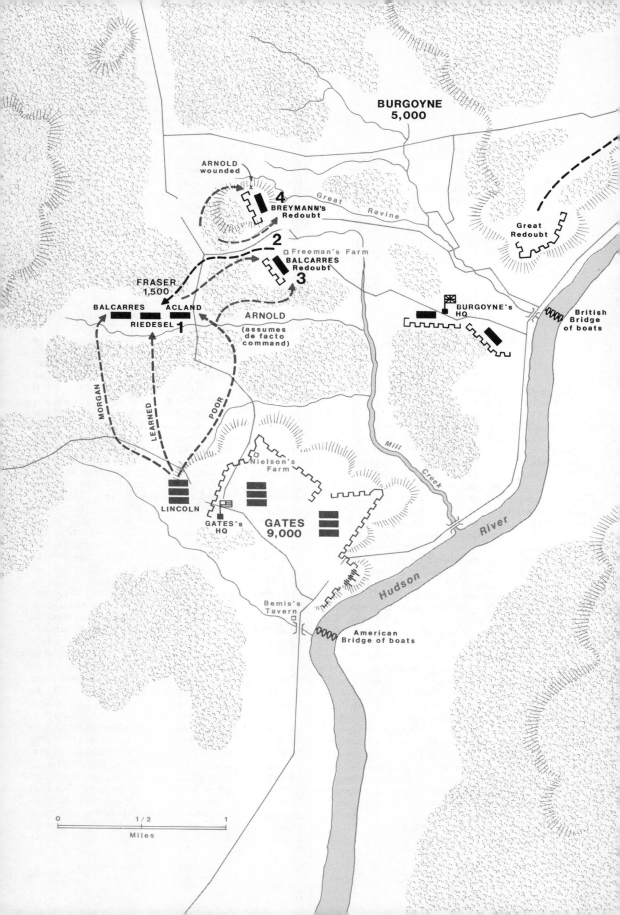

BURGOYNE
5,000

ARNOLD
wounded

4
BREYMANN's
Redoubt

Great

Ravine

Great
Redoubt

2

Freeman's Farm

BALCARRES
Redoubt

FRASER
1,500

3

BALCARRES   ACLAND

RIEDESEL   1

ARNOLD

(assumes
de facto
command)

BURGOYNE's
HQ

British
Bridge
of boats

MORGAN

LEARNED

POOR

Mill

Creek

Nielson's
Farm

LINCOLN

GATES's
HQ

GATES
9,000

River

Hudson

Bemis's
Tavern

American
Bridge of boats

0   1/2   1
Miles

MAP # 18

Bemis Heights

October 7, 1777

Two days before Sir Henry Clinton attacked the American forts on the Hudson, Burgoyne called a council of war of his senior officers. The British situation was grim. Virtually abandoned now by its Indian allies and many of the Tory sympathizers, the British army had suffered serious losses in two battles, and numbered no more than 5,000. Supplies were running out, and the number of sick and missing was increasing. Nevertheless at the council of war, Burgoyne urged an all-out offensive against the American position. His officers demurred. They pointed out that the thick forest made it impossible for the British to obtain any information at all about the American strength or disposition. Burgoyne therefore suggested a reconnaissance in force to find the American left and test its strength. If the situation appeared promising, the reconnaissance could be expanded into a full attack.

The only thing working in Burgoyne's favor in this plan was the growing enmity between the American Generals Gates and Arnold. Gates had become jealous of the glory Arnold had won at Freeman's Farm, and sought revenge by refusing to mention Arnold's name in his formal dispatches to Congress. Arnold protested this slight to Gates in person and Gates took the opportunity to relieve his most effective subordinate of command, replacing him with Major General Benjamin Lincoln.

On the morning of October 7, General Simon Fraser led some 1,500 men in three columns from the British fortifications at Freeman's Farm. They advanced about three quarters of a mile to the edge of Barber's wheatfield (1) where they deployed. As a reconnaisance it was a complete failure, for nothing could be seen of the American lines. But the Americans had seen them, and Gates sent out Morgan's rifleman to, as he put it, "start the game." Morgan and Dearborn assailed the British right composed of the light infantry companies under Major Lord Balcarres, while Enoch Poor's brigade of some 800 men attacked the British left composed of the grenadiers under Major John Dyke Acland. The British were out of

their element fighting in the rough terrain of Mill Creek and both flanks gave way, exposing Riedesel's Germans to the attack of Learned's brigade.

Unable to stay away when he heard the sound of battle, Benedict Arnold spurred onto the field just as Learned's brigade began its assault. Though tgechnically he was without authority, the men cheered his arrival and he called to them to follow him which they did with enthusiasm. Riedelsel's veterans, their flanks exposed, could not stand up to the fury of Arnold's attack and they too fell back. The American attack was unrelenting and when Fraser tried to form a second line of defense, one of Morgan's marksmen felled him. The British and Germans fled back to their prepared defenses around Freeman's Farm (2).

The British reconnaissance had been repulsed with heavy losses, but Arnold's blood was up now and he called to the men to assault the enemy breastworks. The first strong point in their path was Balcarres' redoubt (3). The initial American assault was driven back, but the Americans worked their way around the flanks and took the fort from the rear. The Germans threw down their arms or fled. Arnold galloped onward to Breymann's redoubt (4). As he organized an assault on the strong point, he was shot in the leg — the same leg where he had been wounded at Quebec — and while he lay on the ground, a messenger from Gates arrived to tell him that he was not allowed on the field. Too late: the battle was over. Thanks largely to Arnold's leadership, the Americans had seized both Balcarres' and Breymann's redoubts and thereby had rendered the entire British position untenable. Moreover, both Fraser and Breymann had been mortally wounded, the British had lost another 600 men, and their morale was shattered. The Americans had lost only 150, though one of them was Arnold. Gates had not budged from the fortifications on Bemis Heights.

Burgoyne's options now narrowed to one. He had to retreat if he could. Abandoning their sick and wounded, the British began to slog northward up the river road (5) on the evening of October 8. Their progress was slow and they did not reach the high ground around the village of Saratoga until the next evening. There Burgoyne called another conference of his officers. They voted to continue to attempt to fight their way northward toward Fort Edward. Burgoyne initially agreed, but the next day he countermanded the orders. Instead he sought the approval of his officers to open negotiations with Gates for the surrender of the army.

In this, at least, Burgoyne bested his American counterpart, for instead of a surrender, Gates accepted Burgoyne's suggestion of a "convention" in which the Americans agreed to allow the British to return to England in exchange for a promise that they would not fight again in the war. Congress later disavowed this agreement and Burgoyne's unfortunate soldiers would instead be interned in prison camps in Virginia until the end of the war.

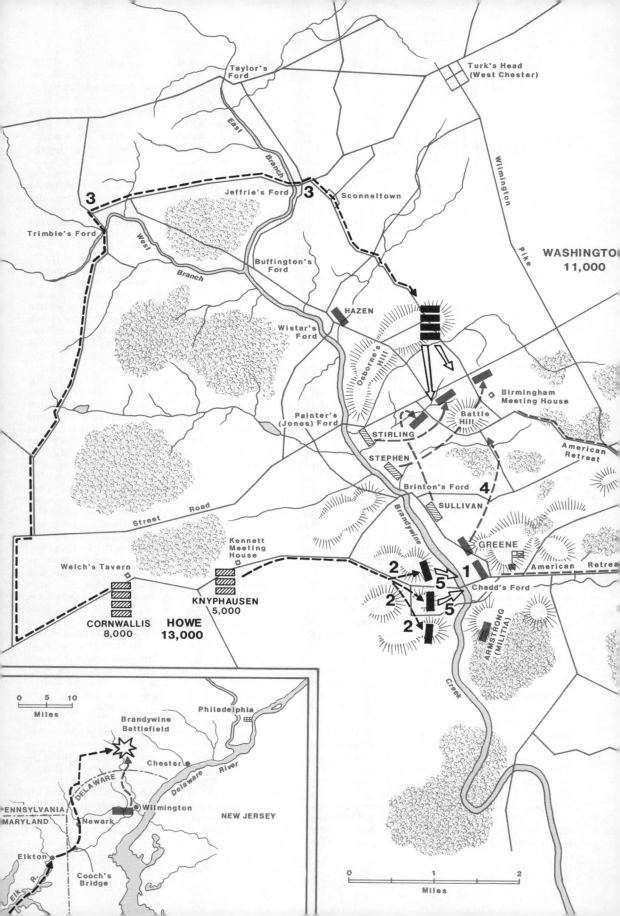

Taylor's Ford

Turk's Head
(West Chester)

East Branch

3

Jeffrie's Ford **3** Sconneltown

Trimble's Ford

West Branch

Buffington's Ford

WASHINGTO
11,000

Wilmington Pike

Wistar's Ford

HAZEN

Osborne's Hill

Birmingham
Meeting House

Painter's
(Jones) Ford

Battle
Hill

STIRLING

American
Retreat

STEPHEN

Brinton's Ford **4**

SULLIVAN

Street Road

GREENE

American Retrea

Kennett
Meeting
House

2

5

1

Chadd's Ford

Welch's Tavern

KNYPHAUSEN
5,000

2

5

2

ARMSTRONG
(MILITIA)

CORNWALLIS
8,000

HOWE
13,000

Creek

0   5   10
Miles

Philadelphia

Brandywine
Battlefield

Chester

Delaware River

DELAWARE

PENNSYLVANIA
MARYLAND

Newark

Wilmington

NEW JERSEY

Elkton

Elk R.

Cooch's
Bridge

0   1   2
Miles

MAP # 19

Brandywine

September 11, 1777

While Burgoyne's men were hacking out a road from Fort Ann to the Hudson, Sir William Howe was planning a campaign of his own against the American capital city of Philadelphia. Historians have often characterized Howe's movement to Philadelphia as an abandonment of Burgoyne. A few have gone so far as to hint that Howe was jealous of Burgoyne and that he sailed to Philadelphia hoping that Burgoyne would fail. But it is possible that Howe honestly believed that by drawing Washington away from the Hudson, he was doing the most he could for Burgoyne. Washington might otherwise have been tempted to hold the Hudson River highlands with a portion of his army and take the rest northward to Albany to dispose of Burgoyne, and then return down the Hudson River Valley to attack New York with the combined American armies. Finally, if there is blame to be alloted at all, it belongs to Lord George Germain, the British Colonial Secretary, who coordinated British strategy from London and who approved Howe's proposal.

Howe left New York on July 23, 1777 with his 13,000 man army embarked on some 260 ships. The fleet reached the Delaware Bay on July 29 (the same day that Burgoyne reached Fort Edward), but receiving false intelligence that Washington's army was in the vicinity, Howe sailed for the Chesapeake Bay. Having spent more than a month at sea, his men finally disembarked at the Head of Elk (see inset) on August 25.

For his part, Washington never seriously considered going north after Burgoyne. Just as he had believed it to be politically necessary to fight for New York, he now felt it necessary to fight for Philadelphia, the seat of Congress and the *de facto* capital of the new nation. His army of Continentals numbered 8,000, but he also had some 3,000 Pennsylvania militia. Washington sent small detachments ahead to "hang on" to Howe's army and perform the double service of harassing the British on the march and keeping him informed of Howe's progress. Sharp skirmishing occurred at Elkton on August 28, at Wilmington on August 31, and at Cooch's Bridge, Delaware on September 3 (see inset).

Washington made his stand along the banks of the Brandywine Creek about halfway to Philadelphia. The stream could be crossed only at a few widely spaced fords. Washington placed Greene's division, arguably his best troops, at Chadd's Ford (1) on the main road to Philadelphia, the Pennsylvania militia under General John Armstrong on the left near Pyle's Ford, and Sullivan with Stirling's and Stephen's divisions on the right athwart Brinton's Ford and Painter's Ford. A small detachment under Colonel Moses Hazen guarded Wister's Ford.

Tactically, the Battle of Brandywine was a replica of the battle for Long Island (see MAP # 8). Howe ordered a feint against the American center to fix it in position, then led the bulk of his army on a flank march to the American rear. To execute the feint Lieutenant General Wilhelm von Knyphausen's men drove in the American pickets west of the river, advanced to the high ground above Chadd's Ford and opened a desultory artillery attack (2). Howe and Cornwallis, meanwhile, marched around the American right flank crossing at unguarded fords (3) to seize the high ground of Osbourne's Hill behind the American right flank. Reports from Hazen and others that the British were attempting a flanking movement led Washington to consider an attack of his own against Knyphausen, but a single contradictory report convinced him that the earlier reports were false. He therefore held his position on the Brandywine until Howe's troops appeared on Osborne's Hill. Typically, however, Howe hesitated before launching the blow that might have destroyed Washington's army. His delay gave Sullivan time to pivot his forces ninety degrees, refusing his flank to face the new threat. In addition, Washington ordered Greene's division to be ready to move if Sullivan's men failed to hold.

At four o'clock, twelve hours after they had begun their flank march, Howe's men attacked. One of Sullivan's brigades gave way almost immediately and Washington ordered Greene to march to his aid (4). Greene's men performed a prodigy of marching, covering four miles in 45 minutes in the blazing heat to arrive in time to save Sullivan from destruction. Nevertheless, the British pushed the Americans back in an hour and a half of fierce hand-to-hand fighting on Battle Hill. Upon hearing the sounds of battle, Knyphausen launched an attack of his own (5) against the weakened American center and it too gave way, the Germans capturing most of Washington's artillery. There was nothing for Washington to do now but break off the fight and escape eastward (6).

Casualties were heavy: the Americans lost a thousand men in all categories, the British about half as many. Neither commander had distinguished himself. Washington had committed a serious error by leaving his right flank open, and Howe had demonstrated his customary lack of decisiveness. Howe had won the day, but once again he had allowed Washington's army to escape.

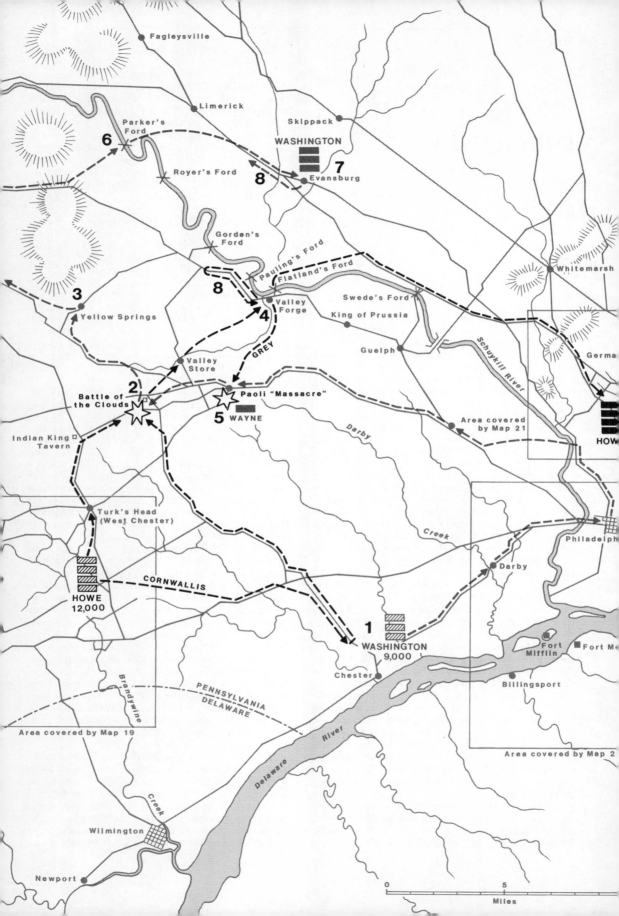

Fagleysville

Limerick

Skippack

Parker's
Ford

6

Royer's Ford

WASHINGTON

7

8

Evansburg

Gorden's
Ford

Pauling's Ford

Flatland's Ford

8

Swede's Ford

Whitemarsh

3

Valley
Forge

King of Prussia

Germa

Yellow Springs

Valley
Store

4

GREY

Guelph

Schuylkill River

Battle of
the Clouds

2

Paoli "Massacre"

5 WAYNE

Darby

Area covered
by Map 21

HOW

Indian King
Tavern

Turk's Head
(West Chester)

Creek

Philadelph

CORNWALLIS

HOWE
12,000

Darby

1 WASHINGTON
9,000

Fort
Mifflin

Fort M

Chester

Billingsport

Brandywine

PENNSYLVANIA
DELAWARE

Area covered by Map 19

Delaware

River

Area covered
by Map 2

Creek

Wilmington

Newport

0   5

Miles

MAP # 20

The Paoli "Massacre"

September 21, 1777

After his defeat at Brandywine, Washington withdrew to Chester (1) to reorganize, then marched via Philadelphia to a position some twenty miles west of the city near White Horse Tavern (2) in order to guard the fords of the Schuykill River. Much more than the Brandywine, the Schuykill was a significant barrier to any army and Howe would have to cross it to attain his goal.

Leisurely as usual, Howe waited a day before sending Cornwallis in pursuit, then four days later he set his army in motion northward through Turk's Head (now West Chester) to clash with Washington's army on September 16 two miles south of the American camp. The British had much the better of the battle, and were threatening both American flanks when a torrential downpour halted the battle and perhaps saved Washington's army from a catastrophic defeat. Following this "Battle of the Clouds" as it came to be called, Washington retreated west to Yellow Springs (3) then even further west to Warwick Furnace (off the map to the left) to obtain dry powder and other supplies.

Howe, meanwhile, dispatched a column to seize the small American supply depot at Valley Forge (4) where the British set up camp. With Washington's main army so far from the Schuykill fords, Howe was in a position to make a dash for Philadelphia. But Washington had left Brigadier General "Mad Anthony" Wayne and 1,500 men behind near Paoli Tavern (5) to fall upon Howe's baggage train. Learning of Wayne's whereabouts from captured messages and Tory spies, Howe determined to launch a surprise night attack on Wayne's camp.

Howe assigned the mission to 5,000 men under the command of Major General Charles Grey, and ordered Grey to make the attack with bayonets only. In order to ensure surprise, Grey ordered his men to take the flints out of their muskets so that no accidental firings would alert the American sentries. For that order, Grey earned the nickname of "no flint" Grey. Grey's column set out on September 20. On the same day the Continental Congress fled Philadelphia to reconvene in York, Pennsylvania. Also on that day Wayne wrote to Washington that the British were very quiet in their camp. "I believe he [Howe] knows nothing of my situation," Wayne wrote. He was about to find out how wrong he was.

The British column approached the American camp at one o'clock in the morning of September 21. Wayne had pickets out, but the British drove them in and charged into the American camp before Wayne could organize an effective resistance. A popular opinion afterward was that the British had learned the American countersign from a Tory spy. In any case, the Americans were caught completely unprepared for battle. Though Wayne had his men up and on the move in a matter of moments, in the confusion orders were misunderstood. Lieutenant Colonel Richard Humpton, who commanded the American rear guard, twice faced his men in the wrong direction and had to be set straight. In the meantime, the British could see the Americans clearly, silhouetted by the light of their own campfires. Grey's men smashed into the American camp and employed their bayonets with grim effect. In close action, the bayonet was a fearful weapon. Many of the Americans did not have bayonets and they had little opportunity to reload in the wild melee that ensued. One British soldier remembered afterward that "I stuck them myself, like so many pigs, one after another, until the blood ran out of the touch hole of my musket."

Fifty three Americans were killed and another 100 wounded before the rest fled westward. The British suffered relatively minor losses of 4 killed and 7 wounded. For that reason alone, the battle has gone down in history as a "massacre." But the name is misleading; the British forces were guilty of no offense beyond one-sided success in battle.

Grey's force rejoined Howe's main body the next day. But Howe's chance to cross the Schuykill uncontested had fled with his decision to smash Wayne's command. Washington had crossed the Schuykill at Parker's Ford (6) and was now at Evansburg (7) in position to dispute a river crossing by the British. Howe therefore employed a simple ruse to divert Washington away from the river. He marched westward toward the upper fords causing Washington to parallel his movements north of the river (8) then he counter-marched at night and crossed the Schuykill at Flatland's Ford near Valley Forge on September 23, a move which put him between Washington and Philadelphia. The British army entered Germantown on September 25 and marched into Philadelphia the next day amid the cheers of the Tory residents.

Washington was painfully disappointed by the loss of Philadelphia and eager for an opportunity to counter-attack and drive the British from the city. Despite heavy casualties at Brandywine and Paoli, he had been able to replace his losses, whereas Howe could not. When Washington learned that Howe had dispatched an expedition against Billingsport on the Jersey side of the Delaware River, he decided that his opportunity had arrived.

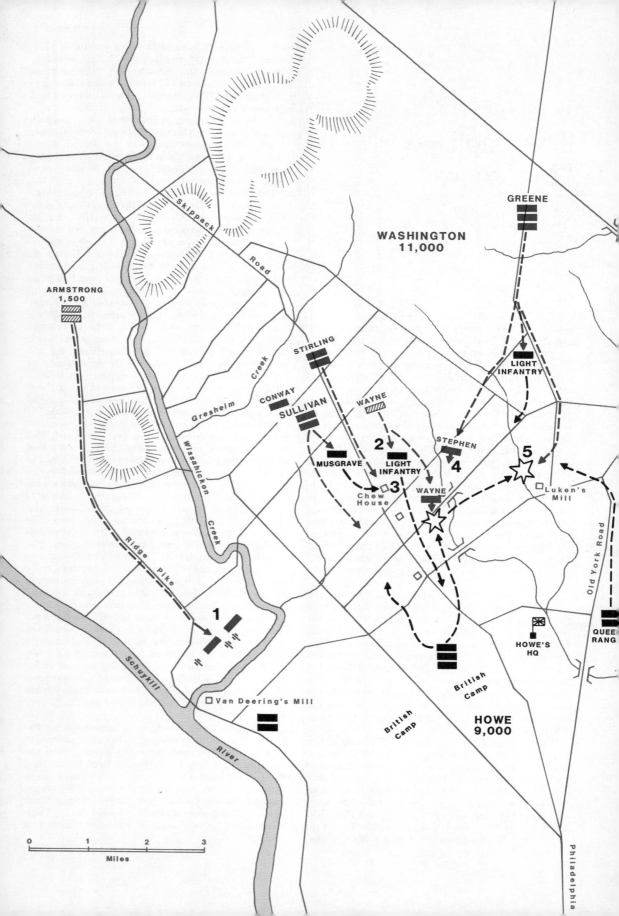

ARMSTRONG
1,500

WASHINGTON
11,000

GREENE

Skippack

Road

LIGHT
INFANTRY

STIRLING

Creek

Gresheim

CONWAY

SULLIVAN

WAYNE

STEPHEN

5

Wissahickon

2

Luken's
Mill

MUSGRAVE

LIGHT
INFANTRY

4

3

Chew
House

WAYNE

Ridge   Pike

Creek

1

Old York Road

HOWE'S
HQ

QUEE
RANG

Schuylkill

☐ Van Deering's Mill

British
Camp

British
Camp

HOWE
9,000

River

0   1   2   3

Miles

Philadelphia

MAP # 21

Germantown

October 4, 1777

Howe had encamped his army in and around the small community of Germantown five miles north of Philadelphia, but he had failed to entrench and his dispositions gave evidence that he considered an attack by Washington's army a possibility so remote as to be discounted. To take advantage of the opportunity, Washington adopted a complicated plan that called for a simultaneous advance by four converging columns. Each of the American columns would move independently, at night, to arrive at designated attack positions by two o'clock in the morning of October 4. If it worked the plan would catch the British in a closing vice, but it required precise coordination over a large territory and therefore invited confusion.

The American army left its camp just at dusk on October 3 for its all-night march. The Maryland militia under General William Smallwood on the extreme left became confused by complicated marching orders and never got into the fight. On the other flank, General Armstrong's Pennsylvania militia advanced along the Ridge Pike to the Wissahickon River (1), but there they were content to fire a few rounds of artillery toward Knyphausen's camp without advancing further. The brunt of the fighting, therefore, was borne by the two wings of Continentals. The direct attack on the British center was assigned to Sullivan plus the divisions of Conway and Wayne, with Stirling in reserve. The American left, which was to fall on the British right flank, was under Greene's command and included the divisions of Stephen and McDougall.

Sullivan's and Wayne's men were in place on time by two o'clock. At four Washington assumed that the other wings of the army were on schedule and gave the order to attack. Five miles from the British camp, the Americans encountered the British Second Light Infantry Battalion (2). The British assumed their attackers were only a scouting party and fought stubbornly until they were overwhelmed and then they fell back pell mell along the pike. The men of the British 40th regiment of foot under Colonel Thomas Musgrave barricaded themselves in "Clivedon" a large stone home belonging to Justice Benjamin Chew (3). The first group of Americans bypassed the house and continued the attack; Wayne's division in particular, eager to avenge Paoli, pressed forward. But when Washington and his staff came up to the Chew House with the reserves under Stirling, Henry Knox argued that it was unwise to leave a defended fortress in the army's rear and convinced Washington to order one of Stirling's two brigades to storm it. William Maxwell's brigade got the assignment. Maxwell's men took terrible losses trying to capture the house. British defenders were told by their commander that the Americans were probably not taking any prisoners after Paoli and that they might as well fight to the last man. Despite repeated attacks, the Americans failed to dislodge the British and the noise of their struggle confused the Americans who had gone ahead.

The critical moment in the battle arrived some forty-five minutes later when Greene's corps came onto the battlefield. Because of Wayne's rapid progress against the British, and delays of their own, Stephen's men came onto the field not against the British left flank as expected, but into the rear of Wayne's division (4). The confusion was increased by the heavy fog and thick smoke that make it "dark as night" according to one witness, and by the fact that General Stephen was thoroughly and obviously drunk. Coming up in the fog, Stephen's soldiers saw a line of armed men in their front and opened fire. Wayne's men, the target of their assault, were startled to find an enemy in their rear, and returned fire. In addition to the tragic loss of life, the incident halted Wayne's advance which up to that point had been driving the British.

The confusion in the American ranks encouraged the British to halt their retreat and counterattack. Wayne and Sullivan retreated back up the Germantown Pike past the Chew House sweeping Maxwell's brigade along with them. Unaware of all this, Greene continued his advance. Unsupported now, his lead brigade was attacked on both flanks and forced back (5). Greene ordered a withdrawal. The British pursued the retreating Americans for about ten miles, calling it off only after a brisk rear guard action at Whitemarsh Church.

The Americans lost some 673 killed and wounded and 400 captured. The British reported losses of 521. Indisputably, it was another American defeat, but there was much in this defeat to cheer the Patriots. Though the performance of the militia had once again been disappointing, the Continentals under Wayne and Sullivan had driven the British veterans through Germantown and had retreated only when they were attacked by Stephen's division. Stephen's conduct was the one great black mark and Washington did not blink at it; he cashiered Stephen and gave command of his division to a promising young Frenchman, the Marquis de Lafayette.

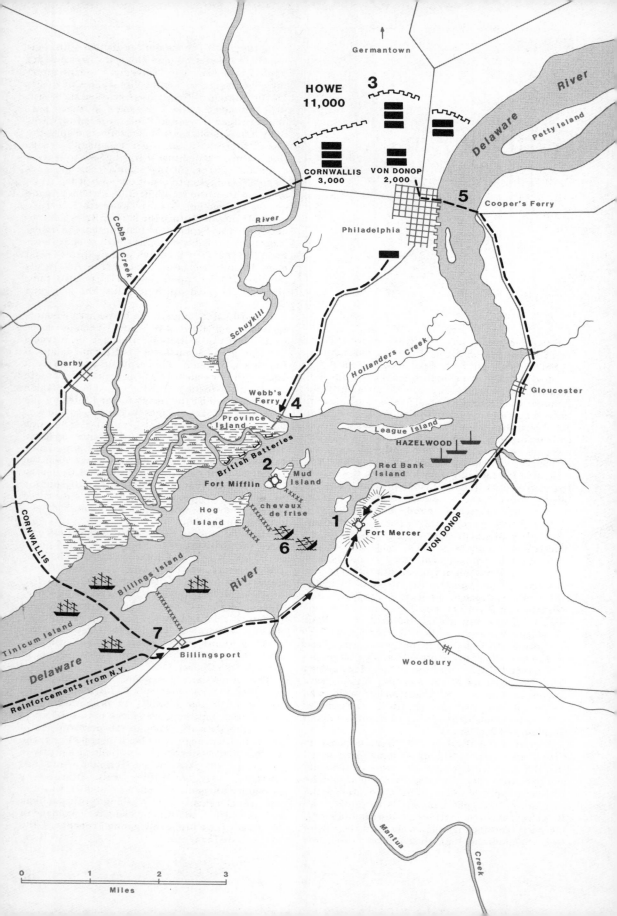

Germantown

HOWE
11,000

3

CORNWALLIS
3,000

VON DONOP
2,000

Delaware River

Petty Island

5

Cooper's Ferry

River

Philadelphia

Hollanders Creek

Darby

Webb's Ferry

Province Island

4

British Batteries

Fort Mifflin

Mud Island

2

chevaux de frise

Hog Island

6

1

League Island

HAZELWOOD

Red Bank Island

Fort Mercer

Gloucester

VON DONOP

Schuylkill

Cobbs Creek

CORNWALLIS

Billings Island

River

Tinicum Island

7

Billingsport

Delaware

Reinforcements from N.Y.

Woodbury

Mantua Creek

0   1   2   3
Miles

MAP # 22

The Siege of Philadelphia

October-December, 1777

When he was told that Sir William Howe had taken Philadelphia, Benjamin Franklin is said to have remarked "It would be more proper to say that Philadelphia has taken Sir William Howe." There was truth as well as wit in the remark. Other than the considerable propaganda value that derived from his occupation of the rebel capital, Howe had gained little strategically and his position in Philadelphia soon became very precarious. After Germantown, Washington sought to make Franklin's witticism a reality by controlling the roads in and out of the city and holding the two forts that commanded the Delaware River: Fort Mercer on the New Jersey side of the river at Red Bank (1), and Fort Mifflin on Mud Island in the river itself (2). So long as the Americans held these forts, Howe's army in Philadelphia could not communicate or be supplied by sea, a condition approximating a state of siege. In addition to Forts Mifflin and Mercer, the Americans possessed a small flotilla of Continental Navy ships on the Delaware supplemented by the Pennsylvania State Navy, all under the command of Commodore John Hazelwood.

On October 19 Howe evacuated Germantown and pulled his forces back to defend the neck of land between the Schuykill and Delaware Rivers (3). By thus shortening his defensive line he freed up a large number of troops for a concerted effort against the river forts. He began by ordering the army to fortify Webb's Ferry (4) and erect a bridge to the south bank of the Schuykill onto marshy Province Island. Hazelwood's flotilla could do no more than harass the British in this effort. British engineers erected a battery on the soft ground and Howe's gunners began a desultory bombardment of Fort Mifflin on October 11. Mifflin's landward face was merely a log pallisade and American guns were either too small or improperly placed

to respond effectively. Over the next three weeks the British continued to expand and improve these batteries.

Meanwhile the British made a concerted effort to seize Fort Mercer. Two thousand Hessian troops under the command of Colonel Karl von Donop crossed the Delaware at Cooper's Ferry (5) on October 21 and approached Fort Mercer from its landward side. Von Donop was eager to avenge what he considered a humiliation at Trenton the previous December and he is supposed to have said "Either the fort will soon be called Fort Donop or I shall have fallen." He planned a two-pronged attack against the north and south faces of the American fort; Donop himself led the attack from the south. Despite their inferior numbers, the American defenders decimated the attackers. True to his pledge, Von Donop himself fell mortally wounded, one of more than 400 Hessian casualties. That night the Hessians retreated to Woodbury and then back to Cooper's Ferry. To complete the British fiasco two British warships coming up to aid von Donop's attack ran aground and had to be abandoned (6). The Americans set one afire with heated cannon balls from Fort Mercer, and the British burned the other. The failure to seize Fort Mercer was a serious reverse for the British. Provisions was already scarce in the city and residents were asking permission to leave the city to forage for food. Nevertheless the British bided their time until early November when their batteries on Province Island were complete. In addition to the batteries on the island, the British also launched several floating batteries. They opened a full scale bombardment on Fort Mifflin on November 10 that lasted for six days and was so intense that the Americans were forced to abandon the fort.

Following this success Howe determined to have another try at Fort Mercer and he ordered Cornwallis with 3,000 men to cross the Delaware to Billingsport (7). Reinforcements from New York raised Cornwallis' total strength to 5,000. With a garrison of only 400 men at Fort Mercer, Colonel Christopher Greene determined that Cornwallis's force was irresistable and before his men were trapped in the fort, he ordered them to abandon it on November 20.

Washington's scheme of starving the British out of Philadelphia collapsed with the fall of the river forts. He was particularly disappointed because he believed that the Americans needed some kind of a victory to boost morale before going into winter quarters. His only hope now was that Howe would venture out of the city to attack the American army in its camp at Whitemarsh. Howe did in fact sortie from the city in early December, and the two armies skirmished in what became known as the Battle of Edge Hill. But after looking over Washington's position, Howe decided not to press an attack and he retreated to Germantown. Anxious now about the coming winter, Washington headed west to take up winter quarters at Valley Forge. Though in many respects Valley Forge was a poor location for a winter campsite, it was near Philadelphia and Washington was determined to remain close to Howe's army and renew the campaign in the spring.

PART THREE

A Global War

News of the spectacular American victory at Saratoga reached France on December 4, 1777. It was precisely the intelligence necessary to spur the French government to move from covert support to open alliance with the American rebels. France formally recognized the independence of the United States on February 6, 1778 and signed a Treaty of Commerce and Alliance the same day. By June France and Britain were at war.

The entry of France into the war dramatically changed the character of the conflict. From an insurrection within one of the colonies of the British Empire, it grew into a renewal of the international struggle between the two greatest powers in the western world, a struggle that had been going on intermittently since 1689. In all of their previous wars, however, the British had been able to rely on a continental ally to engage the French armies while the British dominated the sea. This time it was the British who were entangled in a costly land war and the French who had an ally. For the British, already strained by the expense of the war (a war that was born of a financial crisis in the first place), the entry of France was nothing short of disastrous.

French belligerency forced British planners to reorient their strategy in recognition of the global scale of the new conflict. For Lord George Germain, the Colonial Secretary who coordinated British grand strategy from London, and Lord Jeffrey Amherst, who was elevated to the top command position, it became more important to guard

In command of the Continental ship Ranger, John Paul Jones enters Quiberon Bay on 14 February 1778 carrying with him news of the American victory at Saratoga. Jones fired a thirteen gun salute and the French warships in the bay responded with an eleven gun salute, the customary number for a republic. It was the first recognition of the American flag by a foreign power and symbolized the expansion of the war into a global conflict. Painting by Edward Moran. (USNA Museum)

against French efforts to seize the rich British sugar islands in the Caribbean and the plantations in India than to defeat bands of rebels in the hinterlands of America. The new British military strategy in America, therefore, was one of consolidation and retrenchment.

At the same time that the British abandoned the stick, they offered the carrot. The king appointed a special commission headed by Frederick Howard, Earl of Carlisle, to meet with American leaders and negotiate a settlement to the war. The Carlisle Commission, which arrived in British-held Philadelphia in June 1778, was empowered to make sweeping concessions granting the American Colonies autonomy within the empire and representation in Parliament stopping just short of outright independence. Parliamentary Whigs were surprised and somewhat amused to see the Tory Ministry offering the kind of terms that the Whigs had advocated all along. But by now, of course, it was too late. Neither Washington nor the Congress would agree even to meet with the commissioners, and a few months later, Carlisle and the rest of his commission returned quietly to London.

While the British sought to consolidate their position in America, the American army under Washington demonstrated a new proficiency and professionalism. Thanks largely to the efforts of Major General "Baron" von Steuben, the American army at Valley Forge emerged in the spring of 1778 stronger and more tightly knit. It was also larger. The returns for May, 1778 showed an aggregate of some 13,000 men under arms, more than at any time since the campaign for New York. With this large and well-trained army, Washington was eager to cross swords with Howe once again.

He would not have the chance. Consonant with the new British strategy, Howe's request to resign was approved and Sir Henry Clinton elevated to overall command in America. Moreover, Clinton received specific orders to evacuate Philadelphia to make more troops available for campaigns in Florida and the Caribbean. These orders were terrible news for American loyalists in Philadelphia. Confronted with the prospect of an imminent American reoccupation of the city, loyalists faced a difficult choice: to stay and bear the wrath of their Patriot countrymen, or to abandon their homes and evacuate with the British. More than three thousand of them chose the latter. Clinton accepted the responsibility of transporting these unhappy refugees by sea to New York. But this burden, along with the need to transport most of his baggage and over a thousand Hessian troops whom he feared might desert on a long march through enemy territory, meant that the army itself, some ten thousand strong, would have to march overland through New Jersey. There in the Battle of Monmouth Court House in June, Washington's army would find its opportunity (see MAP # 23).

Though technically a draw, the Battle of Monmouth was tremendously significant. Not only did it demonstrate the new professionalism of Washington's erstwhile "rabble in arms" who stood toe-to-toe with British regulars throughout a long hot afternoon, but it also evidenced the fact that the British Army could no longer move at will through the countryside. Indeed, Monmouth was the last major engagement between the principal field armies. After the battle the British army completed its march to the heights near Middletown and from there crossed to New York City. The American army rested two days near the battlefield, then it too marched northward to a camp on the lower Hudson. By the fall of 1778, the general disposition of the two armies — the British in an occupied city, the Americans outside watching — was thus translocated from Philadelphia to New York. The two armies would remain there for the better part of three years.

The new British strategy left the initiative to the rebels. Washington's primary goal after the French declaration of war was to coordinate a land and sea attack with the French fleet against a major British base, but the logistic, linguistic, and political difficulties of such an operation, with communication as slow and uncertain as it was in the eighteenth century, were almost insurmountable. The first attempt, an attack on the British garrison at Newport, Rhode Island proved abortive (see MAP # 24), as did the Franco-American effort to recapture Savannah (see MAP # 28). Not until 1781 would such collusion prove successful. Other less ambitious projects included an expedition to Penobscot Bay in Maine, then part of Massachusetts (see MAP # 26), and another against the Indians in New York and the Ohio Valley (see MAP # 27). In two dramatic actions that demonstrated the increased professionalism of the American army, rebel forces seized Stony Point and Paulus Hook on the Hudson River (see MAP # 25).

As a result of British passivity in the American theatre, the war moved away from the North American continent in 1778 and 1779. English and French fleets fought in the Caribbean, in European waters (see MAP # 29) and even off the coast of India. The war at sea proved an additional

Many of the foreign-born applicants for general's commissions in the American army had extensive credentials but little real ability. General Baron von Steuben (who was not a general and not a baron) had phony credentials but nevertheless contributed a great deal to the proficiency of Washington's veterans in their camp at Valley Forge by instructing them in the manual of arms and virtually creating a set of American drill regulations. Painting by Ralph Earl. (NA)

drain on British resources. With declarations of war by Spain in 1779 and Holland in 1780, the British found themselves on the defensive. Even the Americans caused the British anguish in their home waters as impudent American raiders pillaged the Irish Sea, the North Sea, and the English Channel. The tiny American Continental Navy was hardly more than a nuisance given the overwhelming superiority of the Royal Navy. But far more troublesome were the hundreds of privately owned vessels — privateers — authorized by letters of marque from Congress to take prizes from the enemy. Operating boldly from French and American ports, these legal pirates seized over 600 British merchant ships, and their impact on British maritime insurance rates added to the unhappiness in Britain with the government's war policy. Finally, the dramatic exploits of John Paul Jones added fuel to the fire of the vocal minority in Parliament that opposed the war.

Major General Charles Lee was much respected by Washington because of his experience as a regular officer in the British army. But Lee failed Washington at the Battle of Monmouth (see MAP #23) and never again held a command in the American army. (NA)

George Rogers Clark's band of frontiersmen had an impact on both the war and on the subsequent political settlement out of all proportion to its size. In his capaigns to Kaskaskia and Vincennes (see MAP #27) he helped America stake its claim to the Northwest.

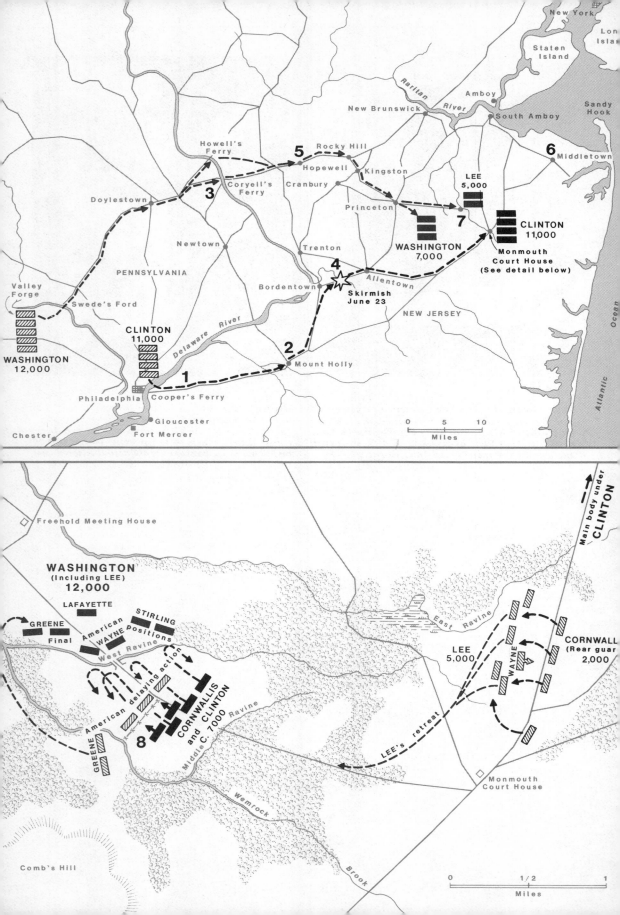

Top map:

New York
Staten Island
Lon. Island
Amboy
Sandy Hook
Raritan River
New Brunswick
South Amboy
Rocky Hill
Howell's Ferry
5
6 Middletown
Coryell's Ferry
Hopewell
Kingston
3
Cranbury
LEE 5,000
Doylestown
Princeton
7
Newtown
Trenton
WASHINGTON 7,000
CLINTON 11,000
PENNSYLVANIA
4
Allentown
Monmouth Court House (See detail below)
Valley Forge
Skirmish June 23
Swede's Ford
Bordentown
NEW JERSEY
Delaware River
WASHINGTON 12,000
CLINTON 11,000
2
Mount Holly
Philadelphia
Cooper's Ferry
1
Atlantic Ocean
Chester
Gloucester
Fort Mercer

0   5   10
Miles

Bottom map (detail):

Freehold Meeting House

WASHINGTON (Including LEE) 12,000

LAFAYETTE
STIRLING
GREENE Final
American WAYNE positions
West Ravine
American delaying action
GREENE
8
CORNWALLIS and CLINTON C. 7000
Middle Ravine

East Ravine

Main body under CLINTON

LEE 5,000
WAYNE
CORNWALL (Rear guar) 2,000

LEE's retreat

Monmouth Court House

Wemrock Brook

Comb's Hill

0   1/2   1
Miles

MAP # 23

Monmouth

June 28, 1778

Clinton began evacuating Philadelphia on June 18. On that day the British army crossed the Delaware at Cooper's Ferry (1) and began a relaxed march through Haddonfield and Moorestown to Mount Holly (2). On the same day, Washington dispatched small groups to harass the British army on its march, and started the main body of the American army toward Coryell's Ferry (3). Washington was eager to bring on a battle with Clinton before the British reached the safety of New York, but not all of Washington's officers agreed with this ambition. Specifically Major General Charles Lee, recently exchanged after a year and a half as a prisoner of the British, argued that since the French alliance meant almost certain victory in the long run, it was unwise to tempt fate by committing the army to battle under any circumstances other than overwhelming superiority. Lee's advice was based largely on his conviction that American soldiers were incapable of facing British regulars in a stand-up battle, von Steuben notwithstanding.

On June 23 the British army brushed aside a body of New Jersey militia at Crosswicks (4) and the American army entered Hopewell (5) where Washington called a council of war. Lee continued to oppose a general engagement with the British and argued his case so convincingly that Washington agreed to abandon the idea for the time being and instead sent an additional 1,500 men to harass the British rear guard. Later in the day, however, Washington ordered another 1,400 men and Daniel Morgan's 600 riflemen — reinforcements that raised the number "harassing" Clinton to over 5,000.

At Allentown Clinton decided that rather than continue northward toward New Brunswick and a crossing of the Raritan where he feared he might encounter Gates with the northern American army, he would instead head eastward toward the high ground around Middletown (6). On June 25, therefore, he started his army on the road to Monmouth Court House. That same day the American army reached Cranbury within striking distance of Clinton's column.

With action imminent, Washington placed Charles Lee in command of the advanced body near Englishtown (7) and gave him explicit orders to attack the enemy rear guard the next day. He further ordered Lee to call a conference of the officers under his command and coordinate a plan of attack. Lee called the conference, but told his officers only that they should be alert for orders on the battlefield.

At about eight the next morning, Lee's advanced body of 5,000 men and twelve guns approached the British rear guard a few miles north of Monmouth Court House (see lower map). General Wayne's division in the lead skirmished with a British covering party, but almost immediately Lee lost command of the situation. He issued various orders moving units from one place to another, but never developed a clear plan of attack and his subordinates became confused. After several hours the Americans began to fall back piecemeal.

Washington learned of the retreat when he encountered the fleeing soldiers of Lee's command. He was appalled. He could not imagine the reason for such a retreat. He spurred forward and demanded an explanation from Lee. That officer had no satisfactory answer except to argue once again that it was not a good idea to bring on a general engagement at this time. In a rare burst of passion, Washington told Lee plainly that he expected his orders to be obeyed. Lee sulked at the tongue lashing and Washington ignored him for the moment as he set about preparing the army to meet the oncoming British who were following up their success.

Washington rallied the disorganized elements of Lee's command behind a hedgerow (8) and the newly disciplined soldiers held this position until the main body arrived to take up positions a half mile to the west. There the Americans met the attacking British with organized vollies of musketry and artillery; after a bitter stand-up fight in the afternoon heat, the British withdrew and, after a rest, proceeded to New York. Washington wanted to pursue them, but in the summer heat, his men were too exhausted. It was in this battle that "Molly Pitcher" (Mary Ludwig Hays), wife of an American gunner who fell wounded in the afternoon fighting, brought water to the thirsty and exhausted gunners and thereby earned her nickname.

Monmouth was really two battles: the disgrace of Lee's skirmish in the morning, and the steadfastness of the Americans under Washington in the afternoon. The troops had proven their ability to stand and fight even against British regulars, if properly led. The one dark spot was Lee's shameful conduct. But he was not at all shamefaced. He asserted his innocence in a sharp letter to Washington and demanded a court martial. Washington obliged him, submitted formal charges, and placed him under arrest. Six weeks later a military court found him guilty as charged and suspended him from the service.

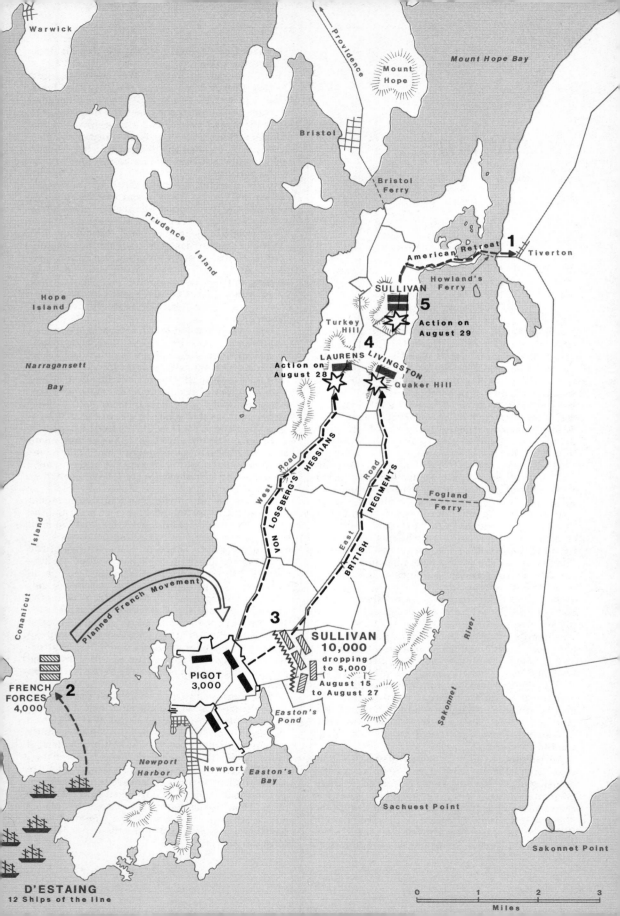

Warwick

Mount Hope Bay

Providence

Mount
Hope

Bristol

Bristol
Ferry

Prudence Island

American Retreat **1** Tiverton

Hope
Island

Howland's
Ferry

SULLIVAN **5**

Turkey
Hill

Action on
August 29

Narragansett
Bay

LAURENS **4** LIVINGSTON

Action on
August 28

Quaker Hill

VON LOSSBERG'S HESSIANS

West Road

East Road

BRITISH REGIMENTS

Fogland
Ferry

Planned French Movement

River

3

SULLIVAN
10,000
dropping
to 5,000

Conanicut Island

August 15
to August 27

PIGOT
3,000

FRENCH
FORCES
4,000 **2**

Easton's
Pond

Easton's
Pond

Newport
Harbor

Newport Easton's
Bay

Sachuest Point

Sakonnet
River

D'ESTAING
12 Ships of the line

0   1   2   3

Miles

Sakonnet Point

MAP # 24

Newport

August, 1778

Washington's great hope in the summer of 1778 was that the arrival of French naval forces would make the British occupation of New York at least uncomfortable if not impossible. He knew that a French fleet had sailed from Toulon in April and in early July he learned that Vice Admiral Jean-Baptiste Charles Henri Hector Theodat, Comte d'Estaing, had arrived off the Delaware Capes with a squadron of twelve ships of the line —large battleships with 64 to 100 guns that were the mainstays of a sailing navy — and that he had some 4,000 French soldiers embarked. Sir Richard Howe's British fleet in New York Harbor contained only nine ships of the line, but when d'Estaing appeared off Sandy Hook on July 9, the French Admiral discovered that his superiority would avail him nothing since he could not get his ships over the bar at the entrance to the harbor. The Americans were unable to supply a pilot who could guarantee a safe passage, and d'Estaing was unwilling to risk grounding his vessels under fire. After discussing the situation with Washington, d'Estaing therefore agreed to take his fleet northward to participate in a combined operation against the British garrison at Newport, Rhode Island.

Washington wrote Major General John Sullivan who commanded about 1,000 Continentals at Providence and ordered him to call out the New England militia. In addition Washington sent Lafayette's division of two crack brigades and later he reinforced Sullivan with Greene's division. Altogether American forces in Rhode Island would eventually number more than 10,000. By the first week of August, Sullivan's force was at Tiverton (1) and the French were landing their forces on Conanicut Island (2) in Narragansett Bay. The plan of attack worked out between the allies was that the Americans would cross at Tiverton and move down the east side of Rhode Island while the French landed on the western side. The British garrison of some 3,000 under Sir Robert Pigot would be trapped on the island because the few British warships in Narragansett Bay had either grounded in an effort to escape, or been scuttled in a vain effort to block the harbor entrance.

The landings were to take place August 10, but noticing that the British had evacuated the forts opposite him, Sullivan jumped the gun and ordered his forces to cross on the ninth. Sullivan's move, combined with the somewhat haughty tone of his dispatches to d'Estaing, cooled the French Admiral's enthusiasm for the project. That same afternoon, a British fleet appeared off the entrance to Narragansett Bay. Howe had been reinforced by a squadron from England and had come north to challenge d'Estaing. The French still had naval superiority, for though Howe had thirteen vessels to d'Estaing's twelve, the French ships were larger and had a greater weight of broadside. Upon sighting the British, therefore, d'Estaing reembarked his troops and sailed out to meet Howe. Hoping to gain the weather gage, Howe bore away on the port tack and prayed for a shift in the wind. D'Estaing followed, and the two fleets disappeared over the horizon.

On Rhode Island, meanwhile, Sullivan advanced to within a mile of the British fortifications and established regular siege lines (3), though he concentrated on the eastern side of the island assuming that the French would occupy the western approaches when they returned. But when the French fleet straggled back into Narragansett Bay on the 19th and 20th, d'Estaing informed Sullivan that a powerful gale had battered both fleets before they could come to grips with one another, and that his fleet now needed to return to Boston to refit.

Sullivan was stunned. He and Lafayette pleaded with d'Estaing to wait, if only for a few days. But the French admiral had become disillusioned with Sullivan and he did not want to be trapped in the Bay if another English fleet appeared. He sailed for Boston at midnight on August 21.

The Americans might have taken Newport unaided by the French, but when d'Estaing left so did most of the American militia. In a few days Sullivan had fewer than 5,000 men. He fell back to new positions (4) on August 28 and Pigot sortied out of Newport to attack him on August 28 and 29 in what became known as the Battle of Rhode Island. On the 28th, Pigot's regulars drove the advanced units of Colonels John Laurens and Henry Livingston from their positions, but the next day they ran into well-aimed volleys from General John Glover's Massachusetts brigade on Butts Hill (5) and were themselves driven back. The Americans rallied and held off the British attacks for the rest of the afternoon. The next night the Americans retreated safely back to Tiverton only a day ahead of 4,000 British reinforcements under Clinton himself.

The collapse of the campaign against Newport was a great disappointment for the Americans. Sullivan lashed out publicly at d'Estaing and all but accused him of cowardice for abandoning the siege. Washington was also greatly disappointed, but did his best to avoid a rift in French-American relations. There would be other opportunities.

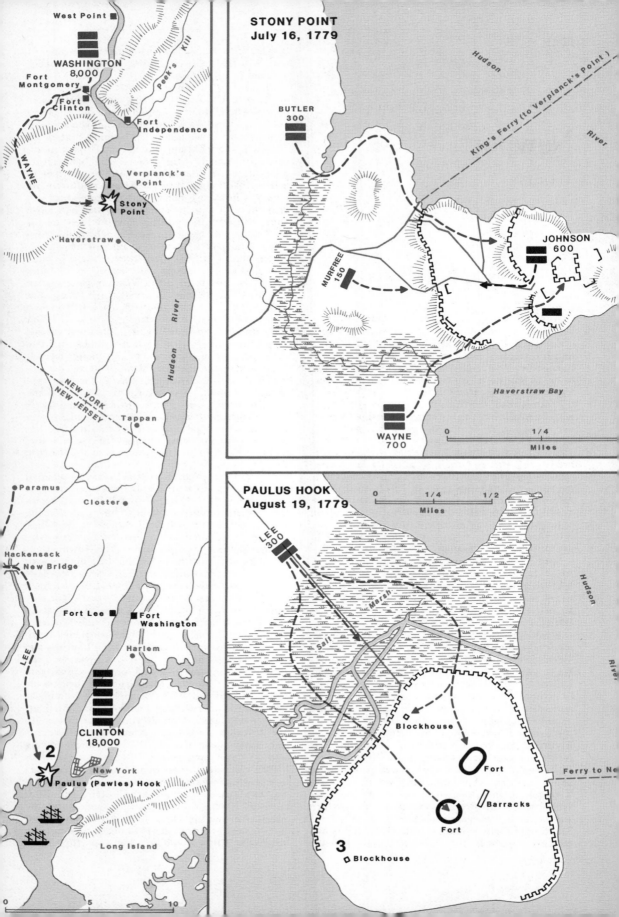

West Point

WASHINGTON
8,000

Fort
Montgomery

Fort
Clinton

Fort
Independence

WAYNE

Peek's Kill

1
Verplanck's
Point

Stony
Point

Haverstraw

Hudson River

NEW YORK
NEW JERSEY

Tappan

Paramus

Closter

Hackensack
New Bridge

LEE

Fort Lee

Fort
Washington

Harlem

CLINTON
18,000

2
Paulus (Pawles) Hook

New York

Long Island

0   5   10

STONY POINT
July 16, 1779

Hudson

River

BUTLER
300

King's Ferry (to Verplanck's Point)

JOHNSON
600

MURFREE
150

Haverstraw Bay

WAYNE
700

0   1/4
Miles

PAULUS HOOK
August 19, 1779

0   1/4   1/2
Miles

LEE
300

Marsh

Sail

Hudson

River

Blockhouse

Fort

Ferry to Ne

Barracks

Fort

3
Blockhouse

MAP # 25

Stony Point and Paulus Hook

July - August, 1779

The British and American armies around New York remained largely immobile for the rest of 1778 and into the spring of 1779. Then in an attempt to draw Washington into a general engagement, Clinton on the last day of May in 1779 seized the American outpost of Stony Point (1) which commanded King's Ferry across the Hudson River, an important link between American forces in New York and New England. The British garrison left behind to occupy Stony Point — some 600 men under Lieutenant Colonel Henry Johnson — called their fortress a "little Gibraltar" and indeed it did resemble a miniature version of The Rock. Surrounded by water on three sides and separated from the mainland by low ground that flooded at high tide, it rose 150 feet above the Hudson to a flat rocky crest which the British stripped of trees and fortified with a series of redoubts. A narrow causeway connected it to the western shore, but at high tide even this was under two feet of water.

Washington at first reacted to the British initiative at Stony Point with resignation. "All we can do is to lament what we cannot remedy," he wrote. But after more reflection, he determined to employ the newly reorganized light infantry brigade of Brigadier General Anthony Wayne in a secret and daring attack to regain the post. Wayne was somewhat dismayed after his initial reconnaissance of Stony Point, but told Washington that he would assault Hell itself if Washington ordered it.

The plan worked out by Washington and modified slightly by Wayne required the troops to target specific objectives rather than mount a general assault. The principal attack was to be delivered by two columns advancing on the extreme left and right, one under Colonel Richard Butler and the other under Wayne himself. A "forlorn hope" of twenty men and an officer would precede each of the attacking columns and guide the way for a second group of 150 men in each column whose job it would be to clear away the British obstructions. Two companies under Major Hardy Murfree were to provide a diversion by attacking the center. Murfree's men were the only troops allowed to load their muskets; the necessity for

silence dictated that the rest would have to rely solely on the bayonet.

Wayne's brigade began its stealthy advance just before midnight on July 15. The right hand column had to wade through waist deep water at the southern end of the swamp, and the sound of hundreds of men sloshing through the muck alerted a British picket who sounded the alarm. The British opened fire from the heights, but the Americans splashed ahead and gained firmer ground. The forlorn hope raced ahead and the ax-men went to work. Unable to return fire, the Americans clambered up the rocky slope and into the British works, the right column only minutes ahead of the left. In thirty minutes it was over; in a wild melee the British garrison was overwhelmed and forced to surrender.

The British lost 63 killed, 70 wounded, and over 500 captured. The Americans lost only 15 killed and 80 wounded including Wayne who suffered a head wound but remained in command. It was a small victory, especially in light of the fact that the Americans abandoned the post two days later, but it was also an important victory because it infused new vigor into American hopes and demonstrated once again the increased professionalism of Continental troops.

Major Henry "Light Horse Harry" Lee (no relation to Charles), who was to make his reputation in the southern campaigns (and who fathered Robert E. Lee), had been assigned to the reserves in the attack on Stony Point and as a result had not shared fully in the glory of the victory. But the operation had inspired Lee and only a few days afterward he proposed to Washington a similar attack against another British strong point on the Hudson: Paulus (or Powles) Hook 35 miles to the south opposite New York City (2). Washington was dubious, but nevertheless gave his consent.

The tactics of Stony Point proved to be just as effective at Paulus Hook. Though delayed by several wrong turns en route, Lee's 300 men attacked at four in the morning on August 19. Once again the Americans betrayed themselves by the noise they made splashing through the surrounding marsh, but, as before the forlorn hope rushed forward, the ax-men did their job, and the Americans stormed into the fort. Only the British commander and 50 Hessians barricaded themselves in a blockhouse and defied the attackers (3).

The British suffered 50 casualties, and the Americans took 150 prisoners while suffering only two killed and three wounded. But there was no time to celebrate. Lee had never intended to hold onto an outpost so close to New York City, and he began his retreat immediately. Alas, the boats that he had counted on to ferry his troops (and his prisoners) across the Hackensack River were not there to meet him, and his tired men had to march another fourteen miles before reaching the relative safety of the New Bridge across the Hackensack.

In a year that offered so many disappointments, the small American victories at Stony Point and Paulus Hook provided a source of pride and reason for renewed hope.

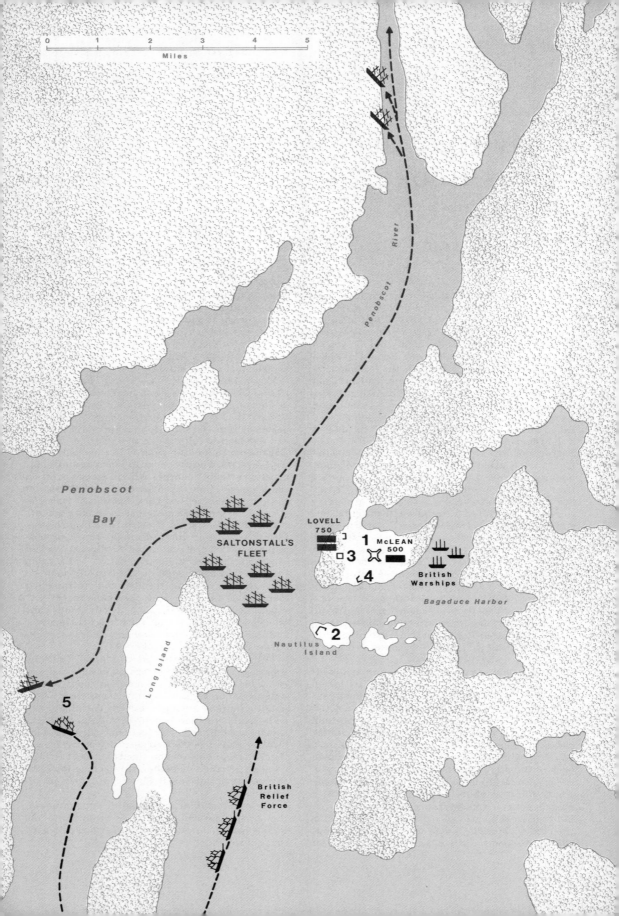

Miles

0 1 2 3 4 5

Penobscot River

Penobscot Bay

SALTONSTALL'S FLEET

LOVELL 750

1 McLEAN 500

3

4

British Warships

Bagaduce Harbor

2 Nautilus Island

Long Island

5

British Relief Force

MAP # 26

Penobscot Bay

July - August, 1779

In mid-June 1779 the British sent two regiments (some 700 men) under the command of Brigadier General Francis McLean to Penobscot Bay on the coast of Maine, then part of Massachusetts. Their goal was to establish an outpost for Nova Scotia and a base for future raids into New England, as well as a refuge for expatriate loyalists. News of the British initiative reached Boston while the Massachusetts General Court was in session, and the delegates swiftly passed a resolution to drive the invaders from Massachusetts soil.

To spearhead the expedition, Massachusetts petitioned Congress for the use of three vessels of the Continental Navy then in Boston Harbor and offered command of the expedition to Commodore Dudley Saltonstall. The rest of Saltonstall's armada of some 40 vessels was made up of ships of the Massachusetts State Navy and private vessels whose owners had been assured that the Commonwealth would make good any losses incurred on the expedition. For the embarked "army," Massachusetts authorities called up 1,000 militia, scraped together six small field guns (Lieutenant Colonel Paul Revere commanded the artillery), and placed Brigadier General Solomon Lovell in command. The expedition departed on July 24 and arrived off Penobscot Bay the same day.

The British fort in Penobscot Bay was located on Bagaduce Peninsula which jutted into the bay and commanded the principal passage into the inner harbor (1). The fort looked imposing to the American militia, but in fact it was a hastily erected dirt fortification whose walls were no higher than four feet. It was completely open on the eastern side, had no platforms for artillery, and indeed was not even occupied by the British until July 26, two days after the American squadron arrived. Despite the manifest weakness of this fortification, the inability of Saltonstall and Lovell to cooperate effectively laid the groundwork for an American debacle.

It started well enough. On July 26 American militiamen overran a British battery on Nautilus Island (2), and two days later they fought their way ashore on the western face of Bagduce Peninsula and captured the high ground behind the beach. But rather than advance immediately against the British fort, the Americans instead began to build a fortification of their own (3) about half a mile away from the British works. For the next several days a stalemate ensued with each side unwilling to assault the other's fortifications.

On July 31 Saltonstall called a council of war, the second that week. At this meeting, and in the several that followed, Saltonstall and Lovell were completely unable to reach any agreement about a plan of action. A full week passed while Saltonstall tried to convince Lovell to attack the fort with his militia, and Lovell tried to convince Saltonstall to attack the three small British warships in the harbor. Lovell argued that undisciplined militia were incapable of assaulting prepared defenses manned by British regulars, and Saltonstall argued that to hazard his ships to the fire of shore fortifications was folly. At their meeting on August 6, the only thing the two commanders could agree upon was to send for reinforcements, an admission that they had let the iniative slip away. Eventually, however, Lovell agreed to attempt to lure the British out of their defenses by a ruse.

On August 11 about 250 Americans sortied from their fort and occupied a battery which the British had recently abandoned (4). From this outpost the Americans sent small parties out toward the British fort to entice part of the British garrison to come out. The lure worked well enough. About 55 redcoats sallied out and advanced "with resolution and intrepidity," as one witness recorded, toward the 250 concealed Americans. So far, so good. But when the British came up to the American battery, they fired a single volley and the whole American detachment, all 250 of them, fled for the safety of their main fort "in the greatest confusion imaginable — the officers damning their soldiers, and the soldiers their officers for cowardice. . . ."

Saltonstall's reaction was his usual one: he called a council of war. This time the Americans decided to try a naval attack. The next day, however, a British fleet sailed into the bay and it was the navy's turn to flee. A few of the American vessels tried to escape through the passage west of Long Island (5), but they were cut off by a British frigate and forced to run aground. The rest of the American fleet fled upriver in confusion as complete as that demonstrated by the militia two days before. As the river narrowed, the Americans ran their ships aground, set them on fire, and fled into the woods. Not a single vessel escaped destruction. It was a military fiasco of the first order. Saltonstall was primarily responsible for the debacle and he was subsequently found guilty by court-martial and summarily dismissed from the service.

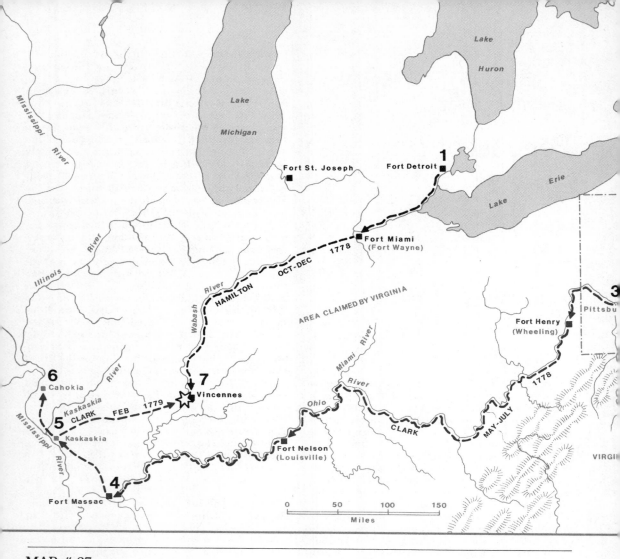

MAP # 27

War on the Frontier

Though British armies rarely ventured inland during the War of the American Revolution, the British did offer encouragement, supplies, and leadership to the western Indians for raids against the American frontier settlements. From Detroit (1), the British Lieutenant Governor of Canada, Henry "The Hair Buyer" Hamilton, sent Indian warriors to pillage the frontier settlements in what is now Kentucky and Illinois, and the commander of Fort Niagara on Lake Ontario (2), Sir Guy Johnston, gave aid and support to the powerful Iroquois in western New York.

The frontiersmen fought back. By far the most important campaign in the West was that of George Rogers Clark. A twenty-five-year-old Virginia militia Colonel, Clark led 175 volunteers on a 900 mile journey down the Ohio River from Pittsburgh (3) to Fort Massac (4) where the Tennessee River flows into the Ohio, then marched them overland 125 miles to the British outpost of Kaskaskia (5) where he completely surprised the British garrison on July 4, 1778, the second anniversary of American independence. From Kaskaskia, Clark pushed onward to Cahokia (6), which capitulated five days later, and then he sent a detachment to take possession of Vincennes (7) on the Wabash.

In Detroit, Hamilton saw immediately that Clark's initiative threatened British leadership in the entire western region, and in October he personally led an expedition of 500 men to recapture Vincennes, which fell to the British in December. As soon as he heard of the British recapture of

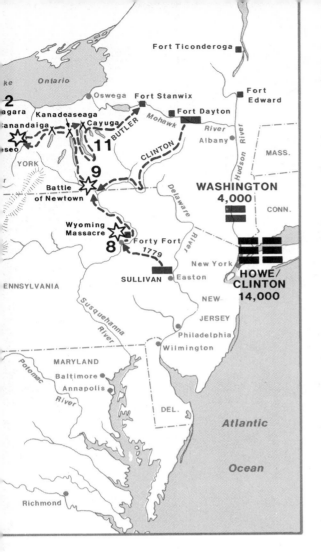

Vincennes, though it was in the depths of winter, Clark set out with 180 men to retake it. After a harrowing mid-winter march, Clark's frontiersmen stormed the fort (which the British had renamed Fort Sackville) and captured the British garrison including Hamilton himself who was sent to jail in Williamsburg. Clark's expedition was one of the most dramatic chapters of the Revolutionary War and Clark is fairly credited with winning the Northwest Territory for the United States.

If Clark's expedition was proof that a mere handful of men could have a disproportionate influence on the course of history, the American expedition against the Iroquois in western New York the next year proved that numbers alone could not assure success. This campaign, led by Major General John Sullivan in the summer of 1779, was marked by widespread destruction of the Indian villages, but achieved little of lasting value.

The Iroquois nation was a confederacy of six tribes — the Mohawk, Oneida, Cayuga, Onondaga, Seneca, and Tuscarora. Conflict with encroaching American settlers predated the revolu-

tion, but British encouragement and leadership during the war increased the level of violence on the frontier. The first large scale confrontation occurred in June 1778 at the same time that Clark was engaged in his expedition into Illinois. From Fort Niagara Major John Butler led 400 whites and an equal number of Iroquois on a raid against the American settlements in the Wyoming Valley, now the site of Wilkes-Barre (8). Colonel Zebulon Butler and 350 local militia marched out from Forty Fort to meet the invasion. The result was the "Wyoming Massacre," a complete Tory victory. Only a handful of Americans escaped alive, and afterward Tories and Indians laid waste the entire valley. Similar raids took place through the fall and winter, and in February 1779 Congress ordered Washington to do something to prevent the continuation of such incidents.

Washington tabbed Sullivan's division for the job and ordered "the total destruction and devastation" of the Indian settlements. Rather than another punitive raid, this expedition was to crush the Iroquois once and for all. Sullivan's three brigades of some 2,300 regulars were augmented by another thousand men under Brigadier General James Clinton and enough volunteers to raise his total to over 4,400 — a huge army by wilderness standards. Unable to confront this huge force, the Iroquois reluctantly abandoned their towns and fell back before the approach of the American army; only rarely did the Iroquois stand and face the invading Americans.

One exception to this rule took place early in the campaign. Just beyond the Indian town of Chemung, 200 British soldiers, an equal number of Tories, and 600 Indians all concealed behind a breastwork, attempted to surprise Sullivan's column on the march. But the Americans discovered the ambuscade and Sullivan was able to execute an enveloping maneuver that drove the allies from their breastwork and produced the only real victory of the campaign in what became known as the Battle of Newtown (9) on August 29, 1779.

Following his victory, Sullivan marched northward through the finger lakes district, burning as he went. At each town, the Americans stripped the fields, destroyed the fruit orchards, burned the buildings, and moved on to the next town. Only once did the Indians catch the Americans off guard. Near Genessee an advance party of 22 Americans under Captain Thomas Boyd was ambushed and annihilated (10). Boyd himself was not so lucky; he was captured and tortured to death.

The army returned to the Wyoming Valley by the same route, though Sullivan sent Colonel Richard Butler east of Lake Cayuga to burn the Indian towns there (11). Sullivan reported that his force had "not left a single settlement or field of corn. . .this side of Niagara." Destructive as it was, Sullivan's campaign achieved far less than Clark's expedition. Though it did weaken the short term military potential of the Iroquois, the long term result of Sullivan's raid was to make the Indians even more dependent on the British for food and supplies and bind them more closely to the British cause.

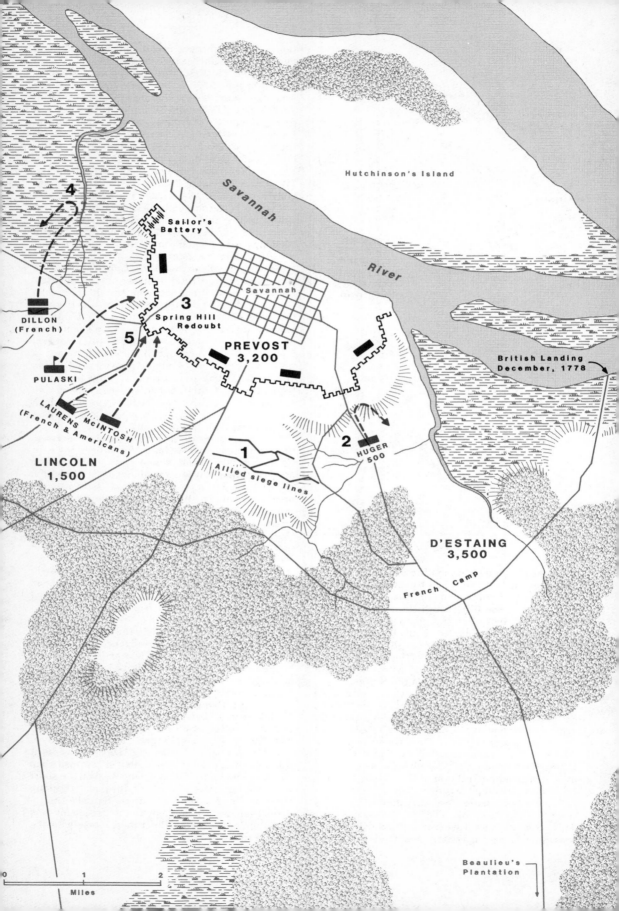

Hutchinson's Island

Savannah

River

4

Sailor's
Battery

Savannah

DILLON
(French)

3
Spring Hill
Redoubt

5

**PREVOST
3,200**

British Landing
December, 1778

PULASKI

LAURENS
&
McINTOSH
(French &
Americans)

**LINCOLN
1,500**

1

Allied siege lines

2
HUGER
500

**D'ESTAING
3,500**

French   Camp

Beaulieu's
Plantation

0   1   2
Miles

MAP # 28

Savannah

September - October, 1779

Part of the justification for the British evacuation of Philadelphia in June 1778 had been the need to supply troops for British operations in the Caribbean and Florida. Clinton was loath to part with a large portion of his army, but finally in November 1778 he sent 5,000 troops to St. Lucia in the West Indies and another 3,000 under Lieutenant Colonel Archibald Campbell south to cooperate with Major General Augustine Prevost in St. Augustine, Florida.

Stretching the letter of his orders, Campbell sailed directly to Savannah, landed his troops a few miles south of the city, and routed an "army" of 850 American militia under Major General Robert Howe on December 29, 1778. The easy capture of Savannah convinced the British that the toe-hold could be expanded into a center of loyalism. Prevost brought another thousand men from Flordia and dispatched Campbell up the Savannah River to recruit loyalist volunteers. Some 1,400 loyalists joined Campbell at Augusta, but another 700 on their way to enlist were ambushed and scattered by a party of Patriot militia at the Battle of Kettle Creek on February 14. This setback cooled loyalist ardor, and news that American Major General Benjamin Lincoln was approaching with an army of Continentals from Charleston convinced Campbell to return to Savannah. En route, he defeated a party of Patriots in the Battle of Briar Creek on March 2.

In June Prevost launched a campaign against Charleston. He called upon the city to surrender, but Governor John Rutledge countered with a suggestion that Charleston remain neutral in the war as a kind of open city. Prevost dismissed this idea, but the return of Lincoln's army sent him back to Savannah after a brisk rear guard fight at Stono Ferry (June 19, 1779).

Recognizing their inability to drive the British out of Savannah unaided, the Americans called upon the French for help. Admiral d'Estaing had taken his fleet south to the West Indies after the failure of the operation against Newport in August 1778, and despite the hurricane season, he readily agreed to participate in a combined operation against Savannah. On September 12, 1779 d'Estaing landed 3,500 men at Beaulieu's Plantation on the Vernon River eight miles south of Savannah and began marching northward. On the 16th Lincoln joined him with 1,500 Continentals and militia and this time it was the allies' turn to call upon Prevost to surrender. Prevost said he needed twenty-four hours to think it over. In fact, what Prevost needed was time to recall the detached elements of his command. Colonel Maitland in particular performed heroics by marching his 800 men from Port Royal through the swamps of the Carolina coast. After Maitland arrived, Prevost answered d'Estaing's call for surrender with defiance and on September 23 the allies opened regular siege operations (1).

The Americans opened fire on the city on October 4, but their cannonade had little apparent effect on the British works and after five days d'Estaing began to worry about his fleet. He now proposed that the allies assault the British works and carry the city in a *coup de main*. D'Estaing's plan called for a party of 500 militia under Brigadier General Isaac Huger to feint against the southeast corner of the British fortifications (2) while the main army attacked the western side. The Spring Hill redoubt at the southwestern corner (3) was to be the focus of the assault. Such a plan might have been a good idea when d'Estaing first arrived, but in the two weeks since, Prevost's soldiers and more than 500 black slaves pressed into the British service had turned the city into a virtual fortress.

The attack took place just after dawn on October 9. Huger's militia found the going tough and did not carry out a convincing feint. More importantly, one of the two attacking columns on the left became mired in the swamps and turned back (4). Only one column, composed of some 1,200 French and the American Continentals, charged across the cleared glacis, hurled aside the obstructions, and mounted the parapet (5). Francis Marion's South Carolina Continentals gained the top of the wall but met fierce resistance and were forced back. In fact, an American deserter had informed the British of the target of the allied assault and Prevost had therefore stationed his best troops at the Spring Hill redoubt. The French and American attackers suffered very heavy casualties. The allies lost 244 killed and another 584 wounded; the British, only 40 killed and 63 wounded. Lincoln wanted to try again, but d'Estaing was unwilling to tie up his fleet any longer and raised the siege.

Savannah was another American disappointment and another blow to Franco-American amity. But the impact of the campaign on the British was at least as significant. The fact that Prevost had been able to march from Savannah to Charleston virtually unmolested was "indisputable proof," to Germain at least, "of the indisposition of the inhabitants to support the Rebel government." Perhaps. But the inhabitants were no more disposed to support the King's government, as the British would eventually discover.

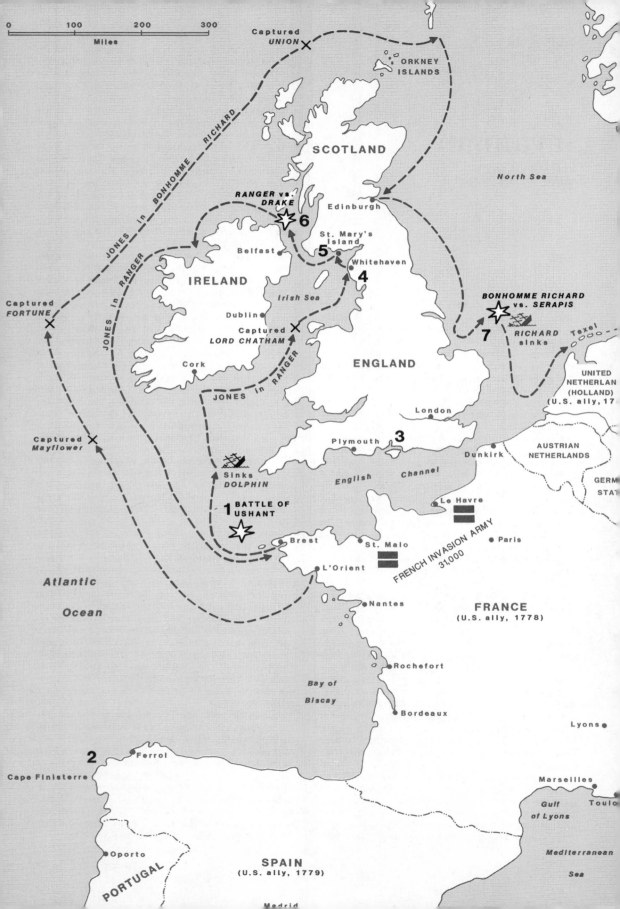

0   100   200   300
Miles

Captured
UNION   X

ORKNEY
ISLANDS

SCOTLAND

North Sea

JONES in BONHOMME RICHARD

RANGER vs.
DRAKE   6

Edinburgh

St. Mary's
Island   5

Belfast

JONES in RANGER

Whitehaven   4

Captured
FORTUNE   X

IRELAND

Irish Sea

BONHOMME RICHARD
vs. SERAPIS   7

Dublin

Captured
LORD CHATHAM   X

RICHARD
sinks

Texel

Cork

JONES in RANGER

ENGLAND

UNITED
NETHERLAN
(HOLLAND)
(U.S. ally, 17

Captured
Mayflower   X

London

AUSTRIAN
NETHERLANDS

Plymouth   3

Dunkirk

GERM
STAT

Sinks
DOLPHIN

English   *Channel*

1 BATTLE OF
USHANT

Le Havre

Atlantic

Brest

St. Malo

Paris

FRENCH INVASION ARMY
31,000

L'Orient

Ocean

Nantes

FRANCE
(U.S. ally, 1778)

Rochefort

Bay of
Biscay

Bordeaux

Lyons

2

Ferrol

Marseilles

Cape Finisterre

Gulf
of Lyons

Toulo

Oporto

Mediterranean

PORTUGAL

SPAIN
(U.S. ally, 1779)

Sea

Madri

MAP # 29

In European Waters

A. *The Battle of Ushant:* The traditional British reaction to war with France was to call out the press gangs, man the fleet, and blockade French ports to prevent the French Navy from getting to sea. But in the summer of 1778 there was a paralysis of leadership in Whitehall, and the French seized the initiative. In July, after the formal declaration of war, Lieutenant General Comte d'Orvilliers took his fleet of 32 ships of the line to sea from Brest, the primary French naval port on the Atlantic. The British fleet of 30 ships of the line under Admiral Augustus Keppel encountered d'Orvilliers off Ushant on July 27 (1). On parallel courses but on opposite tacks, the two fleets exchanged one broadside as they passed. Using new tactics devised since the last war, the French concentrated their fire on the British rigging and succeeded in disabling several Royal Navy ships. The light airs prevented the two fleets from closing again and after nightfall, Keppel took his fleet back into port.

For the British, with their long tradition of naval superiority over the French, the Battle of Ushant was an undisguised defeat, and Keppel, who was a vocal opponent of the war with America, became the focus of the war of words that followed. Keppel demanded a court martial and the court exonorated him amidst the cheers of his supporters. Since the trial had been about the government's policy in America as much as Keppel's conduct at sea, the popular response to his acquittal showed how much opposition there was in Britain to the war in America.

B. *The Invasion Scare:* The addition of Spain to the list of Britain's enemies in the summer of 1779 made possible a combination of French and Spanish naval forces that together could conceivably overwhelm the Royal Navy. To achieve just such a combination, d'Orvilliers sailed south from Brest with 30 ships of the line on June 4. He was joined off Cape Finisterre (2) by 34 Spanish ships on July 23, and the combined fleets sailed northward to challenge the British for command of the sea.

The Franco-Spanish fleet boldly came to anchor off Plymouth on August 16. Anticipating the defeat of the British fleet of 35 ships under Sir Charles Hardy, the French gathered 31,000 troops at Le Havre and St. Malo in preparation for an invasion. But the expected naval battle never took place. Hardy was patrolling off the Scilly Islands when the Franco-Spanish fleet entered the channel, and when d'Orvilliers went out to look for him, Hardy slipped back into the relative safety of Spithead (3). The allies were still in a position to blockade the British fleet and carry out their invasion plans, but the French were low on provisions, having been at sea for three months, and d'Orvilliers returned to Brest in September. Spain recalled its fleet for an attack on British-held Gibraltar and the invasion scare was over.

C. *The Americans in European Waters:* By far the most famous American seaman of the war was John Paul Jones. Jones enjoyed some early victories off the American coast, but made his reputation in European waters. In command of the 18 gun *Ranger,* Jones landed a small force at Whitehaven Bay (4), spiked the guns of the fort, and burned some coastal shipping. He landed next on St. Mary's Isle (5) planning to kidnap the Earl of Selkirk and hold him as a hostage for the release of American prisoners of war. Alas the Earl was not in and Jones's crew insisted upon taking the family silver instead. (Aware that this act betrayed a certain amount of churlishness, Jones later returned the silver.) To cap off this cruise, Jones fought and captured the 20-gun HMS *Drake* in the Irish Sea (6) and brought her back into port as a prize.

Back in France, Jones petitioned Benjamin Franklin to use his influence to obtain another command for him. The best Franklin could do was an old French East Indiaman — a hermaphrodite vessel designed to carry cargo as well as fight. In honor of Franklin's Poor Richard's Almanac, Jones christened it the *Bonhomme Richard.* Accompanied by an American and a French frigate and four smaller vessels, Jones set out on a circumnavigation of the British Isles in August. On September 23, 1779 in the North Sea off Flamborough Head (7), Jones's squadron encountered a British convoy escorted by two warships. While the British merchantmen fled for port, Jones squared off against the larger of the enemy vessels, the frigate *Serapis,* rated a 44 but actually carrying 50 guns, while the French frigate took on the other escort, the 20 gun sloop-of-war *Countess of Scarborough.* Early in the battle, Jones discovered that his larger guns were prone to explode, and he resolved to close with the enemy and take it by boarding. With his own hands he lashed the two together. In a lengthy night battle, the *Richard* was battered so badly that the commander of the *Serapis,* Richard Pearson, asked Jones if he had struck the flag, whereupon Jones bellowed back: "I have not yet begun to fight!" Eventually, damage from an American hand grenade and a weakened mainmast convinced Pearson to strike his own flag. Jones's dramatic victory over the *Serapis* was the highlight in the otherwise poor combat record of the Continental Navy.

PART FOUR

The War Moves South

With the exception of the perennial Indian conflicts, the southern colonies were largely spared the violence of war during the first four years of the American Revolution. But the war entered a new phase in December of 1779 when Henry Clinton led an expeditionary force from New York to seize the South Carolina port city of Charleston. Clinton's expedition marked an important change in British strategy; during the next two years the British would concentrate their war effort in the southern colonies. Rather than an expansion of the war, however, what the British sought was the fulfillment of a hope widely held by the Tory ministers in London, if not by their generals in the field: that with proper support and leadership, the loyalists in America could be made to bear a major share of the fighting. It was commonly assumed that there were far more loyalists in the South than in New England or the Middle Colonies. According to ministerial leaders in London, all the British needed to do was organize and arm these loyalists, and the loyal Americans would win the war for them.

The roots of this new strategy were at least as much political as military. The Ministry of Lord North was in trouble in 1779. The Opposition in Parliament claimed that Colonial Secretary Lord George Germain's conduct of the American war was a failure. The war was expensive, they noted, and growing more so. In addition, so many troops had been dispatched to fight the war that Britain's security was now at stake. The hiring of foreign mercenaries — some 30,000 of them so far —increased the cost still further but with no end in sight. Was it not time to admit that the war was a

Major General Nathanael Greene took over command of the southern armies after the American debacle at Camden in August 1780 (see MAP #32). His skill and perseverence in maneuvering an inferior army kept American hopes alive throughout the southern campaign of 1780-81 and set the table for the American victory at Yorktown. Painting by Charles Wilson Peale. (NA)

mistake? The ministry responded by making the war a moral issue. It would be dishonorable, Germain argued, for His Majesty to abandon the majority of Americans who were still loyal to the crown and who now suffered under the tyranny of the rebels. But how was the government to succor them? the Opposition asked. Every soldier who could be spared was already in America, and after five years of war the rebellion was as strong as ever. How could the war be won and Britain's honor redeemed without bankruptcy? The Ministry's answer was that the American loyalists would win it. All that was needed was British leadership and support. This was the rationale for Clinton's expedition to Charleston and the southern campaign of 1780-81. Clinton himself knew that it was a bankrupt strategy; though there were a large number of loyalists in the South, they probably did not constitute a majority and not all of them were willing to bear arms in support of the crown. Nevertheless it was a strategy to which Germain clung because the alternative was political defeat. It was Britain's (and Germain's) last best chance. If it failed, Germain would have no more answers for the Opposition leaders. The collapse of the southern campaign would mean the collapse of the British war effort in America.

There had been little important revolutionary activity south of the Potomac since the beginning of the conflict. Most Americans in the southern colonies merely wanted to be left alone. When Charlestonians made their offer of neutrality to Prevost (see MAP # 28) they were expressing a genuine hope. But though there was little revolutionary ardor in the South, there were deep rooted animosities among the southerners themselves. This animosity was a product of the political geography of the South. Along the Atlantic coast in the fertile lowlands known as the Tidewater, the descendants of the earliest settlers managed profitable plantations or engaged in the coastwise trade. Of all southerners they were most closely affected by the economic policies of the Tory Ministry and therefore most likely to support the rebellion.

A hundred or more miles inland, the Tidewater gives way to low rolling hills and forests of mixed hardwood and pine. This area between the fall line of the rivers and the Appalachian Mountains is the Piedmont. Here later immigrants, especially the Scotch-Irish, established farms and made a comfortable living, though only in Virginia did many of them achieve the grandeur of their Tidewater rivals. The Piedmont dwellers believed they were ignored or taken for granted by the colonial governments which were dominated by the Tidewater planter aristocracy. In 1770-71 farmers from the North Carolina Piedmont banded together in an organization known as the "Regulators" to protest their second class citizenship. Ironically enough "Taxation without representation!" was their battle cry and the movement led to a small civil war climaxing in the Battle of Alamance Court House (May 16, 1771). The Regulators were defeated, but citizens of the Piedmont continued to distrust the Tidewater aristocrats. Since the Tidewater planters were mainly Patriots, the Piedmont farmers were more likely to support the Tory cause.

West of the Piedmont, in the Appalachian Mountains and beyond along the banks of the Watauga and Nolichuky Rivers was a third band of settlement populated by rugged frontiersmen: the Over-the-Mountain men. Aggressive and independent, these citizens nevertheless desired a strong local government to help them deal with Indian uprisings, and they resented British policies that were designed to protect Indian land claims and limit westward settlement. The Over-the-Mountain men were therefore enthusiastic supporters of the Patriot cause. The effect of these local attitudes, especially in North Carolina, was to create a series of broad bands of conflicting political opinion: Whig along the Tidewater, Tory in the Piedmont, and Whig again on the frontier. That summary is oversimplified, of course, but it does reflect prevalent tendencies and explains why the British could find strong pockets of loyalism in some communities and then be surprised by the strength of Patriot support in others. And it helps explain why so much of the war in the South was fought between Patriots and Loyalists.

Indeed, the first battle of the American Revolution in the South did not involve the British at all. It took place in North Carolina when 1,500 Piedmont loyalists under Donald McDonald marched from the Lower Cape Fear River toward Wilmington. The Tidewater Whigs under the command of Colonel James Caswell met these latter-day Regulators at Moore's Creek Bridge on February 27, 1776. The Whig militia had taken up the planks of the bridge and when the Loyalists tried to cross on the beams, the Whigs blasted them with close range fire and shattered them. Ironically, the Whigs accused these loyalists of sponsoring a "rebellion" and were satisfied that the victory at Moore's Creek Bridge had prevented a "revolution."

After the capture of Charleston, Clinton left Major General Lord Charles Cornwallis in charge of the southern campaign. Distinctly unmilitary looking, he was nevertheless well liked by his troops and unlike many British officers of the day, he was able to plan a campaign in detail and carry it out with dispatch and skill. (NA)

Lieutenant Colonel Banastre Tarleton — "Bloody Ban" to his enemies — led the Dragoon Guards in the southern campaigns. Most feared of all British commanders, he later bragged that he had killed more men and ravished more women than any man in America. (NA)

The shift in British strategy in 1779 brought the war to the South and opened a Pandora's Box of violence. The American Revolution in the South became a vicious civil war fought in large part by bands of partisans. Though the British won most of the set piece battles, irregular militia led by men like Francis Marion (the "Swamp Fox"), Andrew Pickens, and Thomas Sumter harassed their outposts and lines of supply. There were many loyalists in the South to be sure, but the chimera of loyalist support was a lure that tempted Germain with the promise of an escape from his political quagmire. Instead British soldiers in the Carolinas would find themselves in a quagmire of another kind. The southern campaign of 1780-81 that was to be Germain's political salvation led instead to Yorktown and the final humiliation of British arms.

The decisive naval action of the War of the American Revolution was the Battle of the Virginia Capes in September, 1781 (see MAP #40). By maintaining the kind of rigid line-ahead formation seen here, the British settled for a tactical draw that allowed the French to maintain control of the Chesapeake Bay and enabled the Franco-American allies to maintain their siege of Cornwallis' force in Yorktown. Painting by V. Zveg. (U.S. Navy)

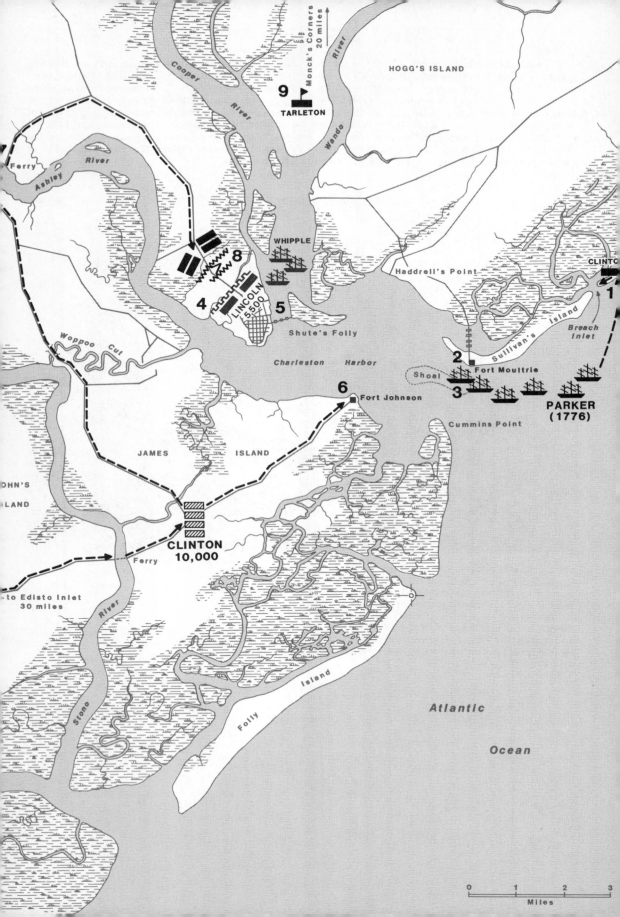

HOGG'S ISLAND

Cooper River

Wando River

Monck's Corners 20 miles

9 TARLETON

Ferry

Ashley River

WHIPPLE

Haddrell's Point

CLINTON

Breach Inlet

Sullivan's Island

8

4 LINCOLN 5500

5

Shute's Folly

1

Woppoo Cut

Charleston Harbor

2 Fort Moultrie

Shoal

3

PARKER (1776)

6 Fort Johnson

Cummins Point

JAMES ISLAND

JOHN'S ISLAND

CLINTON 10,000

Ferry

to Edisto Inlet 30 miles

Stono River

Folly Island

Atlantic

Ocean

0   1   2   3
Miles

MAP # 30

Charleston

Spring, 1780

The city of Charleston occupies the tip of land where the Ashley and Cooper Rivers flow together into Charleston Harbor. Twice the British had mounted campaigns to capture the city, but both times its natural defenses had proved too strong. The first attempt was in 1776, when Clinton led an expedition to Charleston by sea. Clinton's embarked army landed on Long Island (1) expecting to be able to wade across the shallow Breach Inlet (2) to attack Sullivan's Fort (later re-named Fort Moultrie) on the landward side, while Admiral Peter Parker's fleet bombarded it from the sea. But Clinton's soldiers found Breach Inlet impassable and Fort Sullivan/Moultrie with its walls of spongy palmetto logs proved all but impervious to the British cannonade. Two British warships went aground on Middle Ground Shoal (3) attempting to maneuver in the harbor, and a third was hit by American gunfire and set ablaze. The British gave up and returned to New York. In the second attempt three years later, General Prevost approached Charleston from the south by land but his small army was undersized and withdrew upon the approach of Major General Benjamin Lincoln's American army (see MAP # 28). Despite those setbacks, Clinton was confident of success in his new expedition. This time he had both experience and sufficient numbers.

Clinton left New York City on the day after Christmas, 1779 with fourteen warships and an army of 8,500 on board some ninety transports. Cornwallis went with him as second in command while General von Knyphausen remained in New York with over 15,000 men, more than enough to hold the city against Washington's small army. Winter storms off Cape Hatteras scattered Clinton's ships quite literally all over the Atlantic. One transport loaded with Hessian troops washed ashore on the coast of Cornwall in England. Not until the first week in February did the British fleet come to anchor off Tybee Roads. After making repairs, the fleet sailed north to Edisto Inlet thirty miles south of Charleston where the army landed on February 11.

In the emergency Charlestonians gave Governor John Rutlege dictatorial powers and he pressed some 600 slaves into building new fortifications across the neck between the rivers (4). To defend these lines, Major General Benjamin Lincoln had a force of 1,100 Continentals and 2,500 militia, though he was reinforced by an additional 1,500 Continentals in mid-March. In addition, Commodore Whipple commanded an American flotilla of seven warships, but as this squadron was manifestly unable to contend with the British fleet, Rutledge ordered the ships into the mouth of the Cooper River where four of them were sunk to form part of a log and chain boom across the river (5).

Clinton had left 2,500 men in Georgia, and therefore had only about 6,000 on James Island. After seizing Fort Johnson (6) on March 6, he sent for reinforcements that raised his strength to 10,000. With these reinforcements Clinton crossed the Ashley (7) on March 29, and began constructing siege lines against the city (8). On April 8, seven British frigates ran past Fort Mountrie and anchored in the harbor. The city was now all but surrounded, and British siege guns opened fire on the American lines on April 13.

Lincoln's army still had one possible avenue of escape from the closing trap. The log boom across the Cooper kept the British fleet out of that river and an American cavalry force of 500 troopers under Isaac Huger held Monck's Corners twenty miles to the north. But on April 14 Tarleton's Legion attacked and drove off Huger's cavalry, and soon afterward Tarleton and two regiments of British infantry occupied the north bank of the Cooper (9).

By April 19 Clinton had advanced his siege lines to within 200 yards of the American positions and Lincoln called a council of war. City political leaders, fearing abandonment, refused to countenance any breakout attempt by the army. Lincoln nevertheless tried to negotiate an agreement with Clinton whereby the American army would be allowed to evacuate the city, but the British commander knew he would soon have both the city and the army and he refused to consider it.

On May 6 Fort Moultrie surrendered to a landing party of British Marines, and two days later the main British army on the neck was in position for an assault. Clinton called upon Lincoln to surrender. Lincoln stalled and tried to bargain for terms, but Clinton would have none of it and both sides renewed hostilities on May 9. That day the armies engaged in a furious cannonade that lasted into the night. The bombardment broke the spirit of the civilian leaders who now changed their tune and asked Lincoln to spare them the horror of an assault by surrendering the city. Lincoln complied on May 12. All 5,500 Americans, militia as well as Continentals, marched out to ground arms with their flags furled. The surrender ranks to this day as the third largest American capitulation in history, behind Bataan in World War II and Harpers Ferry in the Civil War. Clinton had secured his base for the conquest of the South.

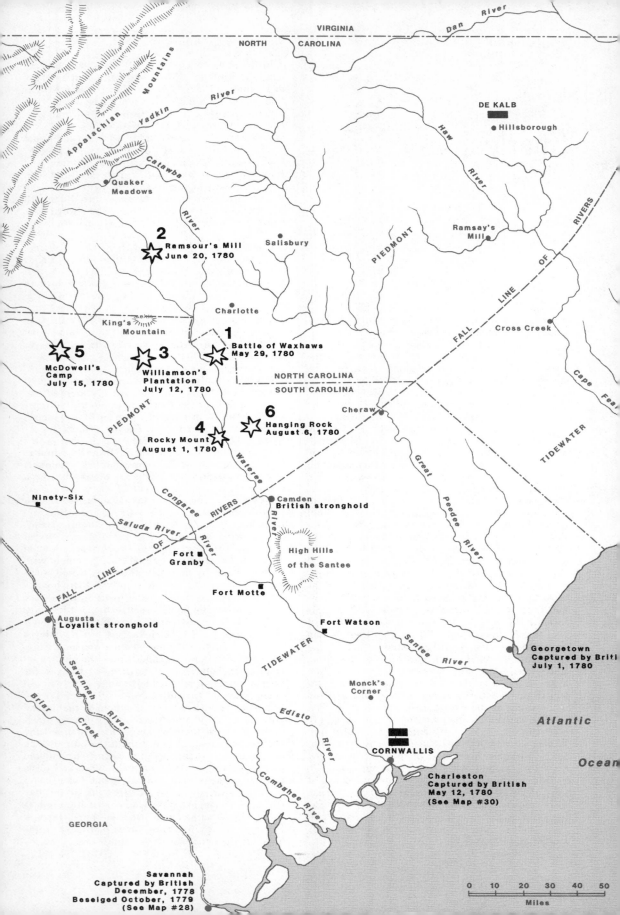

VIRGINIA

NORTH
CAROLINA

Dan River

DE KALB

Hillsborough

Appalachian Mountains

Yadkin River

Catawba River

Quaker
Meadows

Haw River

Ramsay's
Mill

PIEDMONT

2 Ramsour's Mill
June 20, 1780

Salisbury

Charlotte

FALL LINE OF RIVERS

Cross Creek

King's
Mountain

1 Battle of Waxhaws
May 29, 1780

5 McDowell's
Camp
July 15, 1780

3 Williamson's
Plantation
July 12, 1780

NORTH CAROLINA

SOUTH CAROLINA

Cape Fear

PIEDMONT

6 Hanging Rock
August 6, 1780

Cheraw

TIDEWATER

4 Rocky Mount
August 1, 1780

Wateree River

Ninety-Six

Congaree River

RIVERS

Camden
British stronghold

Great Peedee River

Saluda River

OF

Fort
Granby

High Hills
of the Santee

LINE

Fort Motte

FALL

Augusta
Loyalist stronghold

Fort Watson

Santee River

Georgetown
Captured by Briti
July 1, 1780

Savannah River

TIDEWATER

Monck's
Corner

Atlantic

Briar Creek

Edisto River

CORNWALLIS

Ocean

Combahee River

Charleston
Captured by British
May 12, 1780
(See Map #30)

GEORGIA

Savannah
Captured by British
December, 1778
Beseiged October, 1779
(See Map #28)

0 10 20 30 40 50
Miles

MAP # 31

Civil War

Summer, 1780

The fall of Charleston and the capture of the entire American southern army did a great deal to encourage loyalism in the South. Clinton established a string of British outposts across South Carolina and all over the state Americans declared their loyalty to the crown. Clinton's first proclamations were designed to reinforce this mood. He declared that all those who had rebelled against King George would receive a pardon so long as they now went home and behaved themselves. Most Whig leaders did just that. But on June 3 Clinton reversed himself. His new proclamation declared that passive neutrality was not enough. Only those who took "an active part in settling and securing His Majesty's government" would be forgiven. Many men who might have remained out of the war altogether were thereby forced to choose between active support and opposition. Having issued this declaration, Clinton left Charleston two days later and returned to New York leaving Cornwallis in command.

Almost from the moment of Clinton's departure the Carolinas erupted into virtual civil war. The mood was set by Lieutenant Colonel Banastre Tarleton's loyalist Dragoons. Colonel Abraham Buford had been hurrying south with 350 Virginia Continentals and a small group of cavalry under Lieutenant Colonel William Washington when he learned of the fall of Charleston whereupon he began to fall back toward Hillsborough, North Carolina. Tarleton set off in pursuit and his troopers caught up with Buford at Waxhaws (1) on May 29 after a 150 mile ride. Buford rejected Tarleton's demand to surrender, and Tarleton, though outnumbered, launched an immediate attack. Buford told his men to hold their fire until the attackers were within thirty yards, but while such a tactic could be effective against infantry, it was a mistake against cavalry for the Continentals got off only a single volley before Tarleton's dragoons were among them, hacking away with their sabres. Buford raised a white flag, and ordered his men to lay down their arms, but Tarleton's men refused to stop, and the battle turned into a massacre as Tories stabbed and slashed at un-armed and even wounded men. Only a hundred Continentals escaped the butchery. Tarleton's force lost three killed and twelve wounded. Tarleton claimed afterward that he had fallen from his horse and was therefore unable to stop the slaughter, but from that point on Whig partisans spoke scornfully of "Tarleton's Quarter." It was an ominous beginning to a pacification program.

Throughout the rest of the summer, warfare in the Carolinas was characterized by frequent and bitter skirmishes between groups of American partisans rather than by battles between American and British regulars. Neighbor fought neighbor in this brutal conflict and neither side took many prisoners. When prisoners *were* taken, they were often executed afterward, especially if they were identified as individuals who had fought on one side and then changed their loyalty.

One of the earliest conflicts took place at Ramseur's Mill (2) where self-styled Lieutenant Colonel John Moore raised a Tory standard and gathered some 1,300 followers. There on June 20, Moore was assaulted by 400 Whigs under Colonel Francis Locke with another 800 under General Griffith Rutherford in support. Both Whigs and Tories were novices in organized warfare, but though inferior in number, the Whigs had the advantage of surprise. They charged into Moore's camp, and after some close hand-to-hand fighting, drove the Tories from their hilltop. Moore asked for a cease fire, ostensibly to collect his wounded, but during the respite, most of Moore's men took to the bushes.

Another skirmish took place on July 12 when a band of about 350 Whigs commanded by Colonel Thomas Sumter (the Carolina Gamecock) attacked and scattered a party of 400 loyalists at Williamson's Plantation (3). Two weeks later Sumter attacked the Tory garrison at Rocky Mount (4) but was driven off. A Loyalist band under Colonel Ambrose Mills returned the favor on July 15 attacking Whig militia at McDowell's Camp (5) on the Pacolet River. Altogether some two dozen such battles took place between June and September.

One of the most hotly contested battles of this civil war occurred on August 6 when Sumter led 800 North and South Carolina militia against 500 loyalists at Hanging Rock (6). In confused but vicious fighting the Whigs drove the Loyalists from their camp. Many of Sumter's men then became more interested in looting than fighting, and the Tories had a chance to reorganize and counterattack. Sumter's men were driven off, but they had not left much of value behind. Both sides suffered heavy losses; the loyalists lost an astonishing forty percent killed and wounded.

The civil war in South Carolina commanded a depth of passion and a level of brutality not characteristic of other theatres, and horrifying to armies trained in the customs of eighteenth century warfare. A shocked British General wrote home that "these people are beyond every curb of religion and humanity . . . every hour exhibits dreadful wanton mischiefs, murder and violences of every kind unheard of before."

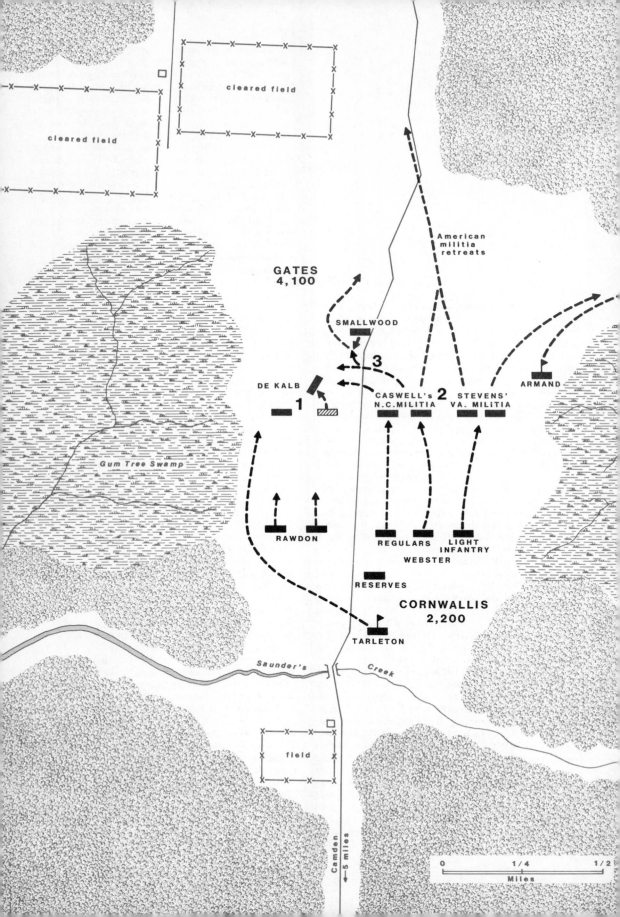

cleared field

cleared field

American
militia
retreats

GATES
4,100

SMALLWOOD

DE KALB

3

1

CASWELL's
N.C.MILITIA

2

STEVENS'
VA. MILITIA

ARMAND

Gum Tree Swamp

RAWDON

REGULARS

WEBSTER

LIGHT
INFANTRY

RESERVES

CORNWALLIS
2,200

TARLETON

Saunder's   Creek

field

Camden
→5 miles

0   1/4   1/2
Miles

MAP # 32

Camden

August 16, 1780

After Lincoln's surrender at Charleston, the nearest Continental regiments were at Hillsborough, North Carolina (see MAP # 31) where Major General Baron de Kalb commanded two regiments of Maryland and Delaware regulars. De Kalb had been in Richmond, Virginia on his way south when he learned of the American disaster at Charleston. He continued cautiously to Hillsborough where he arrived on June 22. With Lincoln's capture, de Kalb became the highest ranking Continental officer in the South. But Congress felt that the crisis deserved a more illustrious savior and appointed Horatio Gates, the hero of the Saratoga campaign, to rebuild a new southern army. (Interestingly, Congress made the appointment without consulting General Washington. Gates was not a favorite of the Commander in Chief because of his presumed role in the so-called Conway Cabal whose object was to replace Washington with Gates.)

Gates arrived in de Kalb's camp on the Deep River in North Carolina on July 25. His "grand army" consisted only of de Kalb's two regiments and Colonel Charles Armand's "legion" of 120 dragoons. A more serious problem than numbers, however, was the dearth of food in camp. The local citizens, disillusioned or intimidated by the series of British victories, were not disposed to offer any supplies. Clearly something had to be done to revive the morale of the army and regain the confidence of the citizens. Gates resolved to advance immediately against the nearest British outpost at Camden where Lieutenant Colonel Lord Francis Rawdon commanded 1,000 regulars and Tory militia. De Kalb was willing enough, but suggested advancing via Salisbury and Charlotte in order to obtain much needed food and supplies for the army. Gates instead ordered a direct march across the North Carolina pine barrens insisting that it was essential to move fast and catch Rawdon by surprise.

The Americans set out on July 27, only two days after Gates had arrived. It was a weary hike. There were no rations and nothing could be scavanged along the way except green corn and unripened peaches. Nevertheless, the American army crossed the Pee Dee on August 3 to rendezvous with 2,000 North Carolina militia under Colonel James Caswell. The addition of Caswell's force doubled the size of Gate's army, but did nothing to solve its logistical difficulties. The march through the pine barrens had further depleted American supplies. To retreat now would lose Gates the continued loyalty of the militia and weaken the morale he sought to build. He could not stay where he was; there was nothing to eat. So he pushed on.

Just north of Camden, with action imminent, Thomas Sumter appealed to Gates for 400 reinforcements to attack a British supply train headed for Camden. Gates agreed though his presumed numerical superiority over Rawdon was not nearly as great as he believed. When de Kalb informed Gates that the American army numbered about 3,500 men (700 more Virginia militia joined the next day), Gates was surprised. He had thought his own forces numbered over 7,000! Nevertheless he sent Sumter the 400 men he requested and insisted that the army was still strong enough for the purpose at hand. Maybe not. Having learned of Gates's advance, Cornwallis had marched from Charleston to Camden with 1,000 reinforcements, thus doubling the size of Rawdon's garrison. Rather than await Gates's next move, Cornwallis started north from Camden to intercept him. The two armies blundered into each other five miles north of Camden on the night of August 15 and backed off to await the morning.

Both armies were hemmed into a narrow battlefront by the swamps along Gum Creek. This should have worked to the advantage of the Americans who had numerical superiority, but in positioning his army Gates made a fatal error. He placed all of his Continentals — his only battle-tested troops — on the right (1), and the Virginia and North Carolina militia on the left (2) unsupported by any Continental troops. When the British attacked the next morning, the redcoats charged into the American left wing and the militia simply dissolved. Many militiamen threw down their loaded muskets and ran without firing a shot. The British infantry wheeled left into the flank of de Kalb's Continentals (3). The American veterans fought back stubbornly though they were now unsupported. De Kalb fought until he fell with eleven wounds in his body, at least one of them mortal. The two regiments of Continentals were badly mauled and the survivors surrendered or fled the field.

The Americans suffered 800 killed and wounded and another thousand captured. The army Gates had inherited was virtually destroyed. And where was Gates? He had departed the battlefield with the initial British assault and ridden all the way to Charlotte. He paused there only briefly before riding on to Hillsborough having covered 180 miles in three-and-a-half days. Alexander Hamilton offered the most appropriate comment: "Was there ever such an instance of a general running away . . . from his whole army? And was there ever so precipitous a flight?"

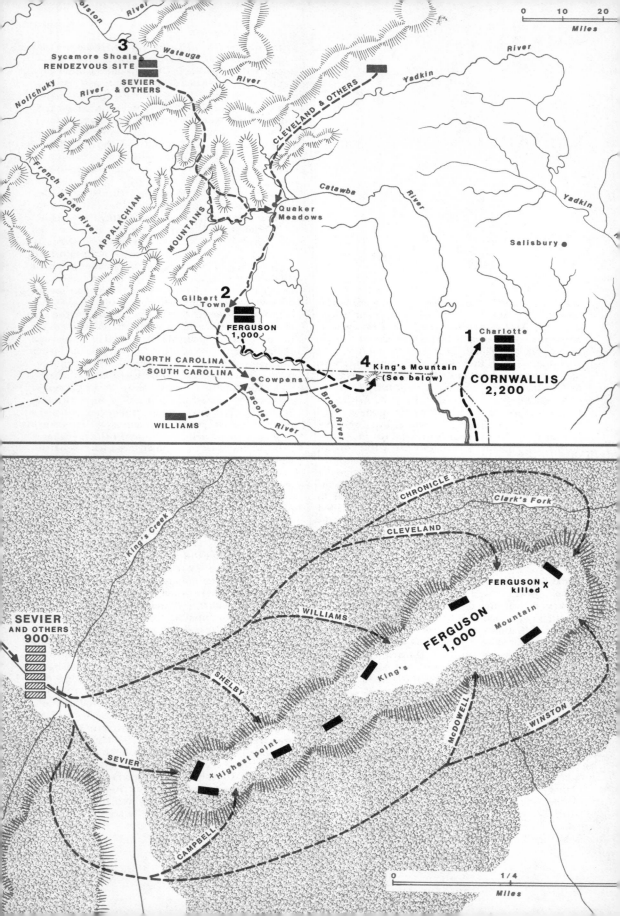

Upper map:

Scale: 0 — 10 — 20 Miles

Holston River
Watauga
River
Yadkin River

3 Sycamore Shoals
RENDEZVOUS SITE
SEVIER & OTHERS

CLEVELAND & OTHERS

Nolichucky River

French Broad River

APPALACHIAN

MOUNTAINS

Catawba River

Yadkin

Quaker Meadows

Salisbury

2 Gilbert Town
FERGUSON 1,000

NORTH CAROLINA
SOUTH CAROLINA

Cowpens

Pacolet River

Broad River

4 King's Mountain
(See below)

1 Charlotte
CORNWALLIS 2,200

WILLIAMS

Lower map:

Scale: 0 — 1/4 Miles

CHRONICLE
Clark's Fork
CLEVELAND

King's Creek

WILLIAMS

SEVIER
AND OTHERS
900

SHELBY

SEVIER

FERGUSON killed ✗

FERGUSON 1,000

King's Mountain

McDOWELL

WINSTON

✗ Highest point

CAMPBELL

MAP # 33

King's Mountain

October 7, 1780

After the destruction of Gates's army at Camden, Cornwallis felt justified confidence that Georgia and South Carolina had been brought under control; he prepared to advance into North Carolina. Of course the civil war in South Carolina continued to rage all around him, especially in the western counties where Whig frontiersmen led by Isaac Shelby, Elijah Clarke, and Charles McDowell conducted hit and run raids against Tory strongholds. On July 30 all three of these frontier "colonels" cooperated in an attack on Thicketty Fort. A week later they struck at Fair Forest Creek, and ten days after that, at Musgrove's Mill. More than a nuisance, these raids threatened to undermine British control of the state. As part of his advance, therefore, Cornwallis determined to throw out a strong flanking column to chastise and pacify the western counties during his march north. To command that column he assigned Major Patrick Ferguson, one of the most promising young officers in the British army.

Unlike most British officers, Ferguson was convinced that loyalist militia could be trained to be as effective on the battlefield as British regulars. It was not his only heretical notion. Years earlier he had invented, patented, and successfully field tested a breech-loading rifle that could fire faster and with greater accuracy than the British Brown Bess. More importantly, it could be loaded while the soldier was lying down. But despite its obvious usefulness, the British hierarchy saw that it threatened the time-tested way of conducting warfare, and they refused to sanction its use. Disappointed in that endeavor, Ferguson took over his legion of 1,000 loyalists determined to prove his other theory. He drilled his men firmly but with compassion and produced a tightly knit and well disciplined unit which he was eager to test against American militia.

Cornwallis began his northward movement on September 9, though an outbreak of fever delayed his advance and he did not reach Charlotte (1) until September 26. Ferguson set up camp at Gilbert Town (2) and issued a challenge to the Patriot leaders over the mountains. Ferguson warned the frontiersmen to cease their attacks on British outposts or he would march over the mountains with his loyalist troopers and "lay waste their country with fire and sword." Such words were more likely to outrage than to intimidate the men of the Watauga and Nolichuky settlements. In response to calls from John Sevier, Isaac Shelby, and others, about a thousand frontiersmen gathered at Sycamore Shoals (3) on the Wautauga, and on September 26, the same day that Cornwallis arrived at Charlotte, they set out over the mountains to teach Ferguson more civil speech.

Learning of their approach from a deserter, Ferguson withdrew eastward toward Cornwallis's main body at Charlotte, but at King's Mountain (4) he turned to face his pursuers. The frontiersmen followed with 900 picked men and arrived near the base of King's Mountain in the early dawn of October 7.

King's Mountain (see lower map) is one of many rocky forested hills in the upper Piedmont near the border between North and South Carolina. It is shaped like a footprint with the highest point at the heel, a narrow instep, and a broad rounded toe. The frontiersmen did not attack immediately for they intended to do more than defeat Ferguson's men; they meant to annihilate them. Led by their various colonels, groups of one or two hundred crept around the flanks of King's Mountain to surround Ferguson's force. John Sevier and William Campbell prepared to assault the high "heel" and the other groups stalked through the thick woods to take up positions around the "ball" of the foot.

The frontiersmen crept up the hill Indian-fashion and opened fire from cover. Ferguson's disciplined troops flushed Campbell's men with a bayonet charge and drove them down the hill. But Campbell rallied his troops once the impetus of the Loyalist charge had spent itself, and the mountain men stole back up the hill and began again to pick off the red-coated Loyalists. Twice more Ferguson's men launched bayonet attacks and drove off the mountain men, but each time the frontiersmen returned and Loyalists continued to fall.

For Patrick Ferguson the circumstances were frustrating and grimly ironic. The inventor of a breech-loading rifle was forced to rely on the bayonet against a body of men who relied exclusively on aimed fire from cover. Ferguson was all over the hill encouraging his men and blowing his silver whistle. But while trying to break out of the encirclement, he was struck by a dozen rifle balls and killed. With his death the Tories began to lose heart and many raised tokens of surrender. Giving "Tarleton's Quarter," the frontiersmen continued to shoot down Loyalists who had surrendered. Finally the several American colonels got their men under control and rounded up the 600 Tory survivors. Those well enough to walk were herded away as prisoners. Some of them would later be hanged as traitors. Though he did not learn of it until several days later, Cornwallis' flanking column had virtually ceased to exist.

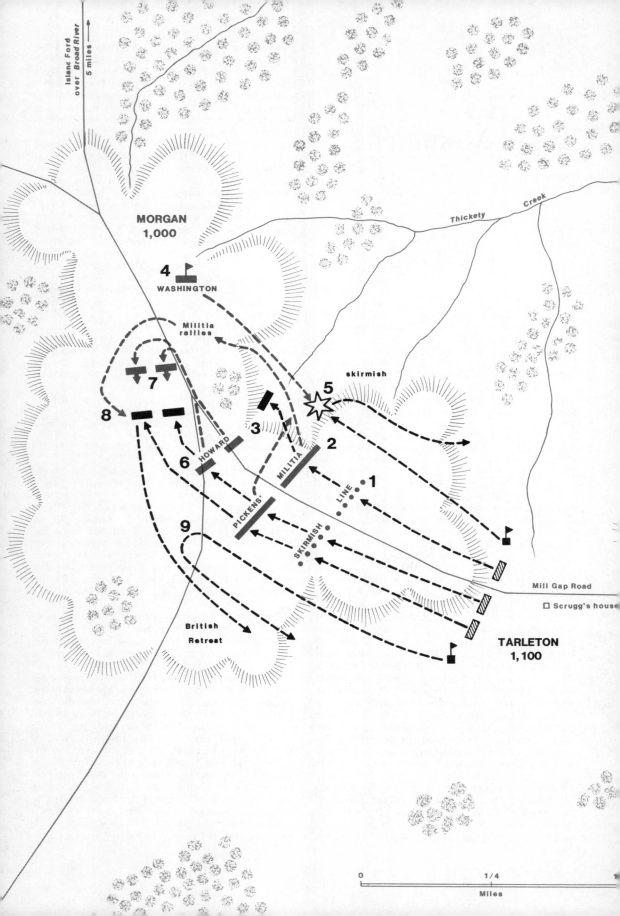

Island Ford over *Broad River*
← 5 miles →

MORGAN
1,000

4
WASHINGTON

Militia
rallies

7

8

3

HOWARD

6

5

skirmish

2

1

MILITIA

LINE

PICKENS'

SKIRMISH

9

British
Retreat

Thickety   Creek

Mill Gap Road

☐ Scrugg's house

TARLETON
1,100

0   1/4

Miles

MAP # 34

Cowpens

January 17, 1781

The almost complete annihilation of Ferguson's force at King's Mountain convinced Cornwallis to abort his invasion of North Carolina and pull back to Winnsboro, South Carolina. Meanwhile Gates struggled to reorganize his shattered command, but his manifest failure at Camden and especially his abandonment of the army led Congress to ask Washington to nominate a replacement. Washington chose thirty-nine-year-old Major General Nathanael Greene.

Greene joined the southern army in Charlotte on December 2, 1780 and assumed command the same day. His army consisted of some 2,300 men on paper; only about 1,500 were fit for duty. Despite his numerical inferiority, Greene divided his forces. He sent 600 men, including Colonel William Washington's calvalry, to the west under the command of Brigadier General Daniel Morgan, and took the rest of his force southeastward to Cheraw, South Carolina, where supplies were more readily available. Cornwallis sent Tarleton and 1,100 troopers after Morgan, and marched his own army to the northwest to place it between Morgan and Greene.

Tarleton started after Morgan on January 6, 1781. Morgan retreated toward the fords across the Broad River, but only six miles from the fords, he learned that the river was swollen from winter rains and that Tarleton was only ten miles behind him and closing fast. Rather than risk being caught by the British while he was halfway across the river, Morgan decided to turn and fight. Pickens's militia had joined him raising his strength to 1,100, about the same as Tarleton's, but hoping to attract a few more militia before the battle, he designated the Cowpens — a well-known local rendezvous — as the army's campsite.

Morgan made his battle plans with great care and attention to detail. The men would be deployed in three lines, he told his officers: a skirmish line of sharpshooters in front (1), a second line of Pickens's South Carolina militia (2), and a third line composed of the Continentals and the Virginia militia under Colonel John Eager Howard (3). William Washington's cavalry would comprise the reserve (4). Morgan doubted that Pickens's militiamen could resist an attack by British regulars for very long in any case, so he ordered them to fire only three volleys and then withdraw. By giving them a specific and limited assignment, Morgan lessened the possibility that they would break and run and in so doing communicate a sense of panic to the regulars. Morgan was not satisfied merely to outline this plan to his officers. He wandered through the camp the night before the battle explaining it to the men in the ranks. Just three good volleys, he told the militiamen, and the girls will kiss you when you get home. Don't worry when the militia falls back tomorrow, he told the Continentals, they are supposed to do that. All night he roamed the camp explaining, exhorting, joking.

Tarleton's Legion reached the Cowpens at seven a.m. after a forced march. They immediately deployed — the light infantry in the center and the dragoons on the flanks — and attacked. The American sharpshooters exacted a heavy toll on British officers, and the American militia fired their three volleys and began to withdraw to the left as instructed. The British dragoons on the right pounded forward expecting to turn the battle into a rout, but from behind the crest of the hill, William Washington's American cavalry also charged and it was the British dragoons who were routed (5). Pickens' militiamen continued their orderly retreat.

The British infantry, meanwhile, having suffered serious losses from the sharpshooters and the militia, encountered the line of Continentals (3) and were halted by the disciplined fire of the American veterans. Tarleton extended his left to subject the American line to an enfilade (6). To face this new threat, Howard ordered his Virginia militia to refuse their right. But the militiamen misunderstood the order and began to march, still under discipline, to the rear. Thinking that the American line had been broken, the British cheered and surged forward, breaking formation. Just over the crest of the hill, however, Howard's men halted, and in response to Morgan's command, faced about. As the cheering British surged over the hill, the Americans poured a volley into them at close range and followed up with a bayonet charge (7). At almost the same moment, Pickens's militia, having reformed in the rear, came in on the British left (8) and William Washington's cavalry hit them on the right. It was over in moments: The British broke and fled or threw up their hands.

Tarleton still hoped to save the day with a mounted attack by his dragoons, but when he called upon them to charge, they refused. In a fury Tarleton gathered some sixty men about him and charged anyway (9). His attack was driven off by the American cavalry and the British abandoned the field.

The Battle of Cowpens utterly wrecked Tarletons' feared Legion. Three hundred British were killed and wounded and another 525 were made prisoners of war. Even more importantly, the battle ended Tarleton's reputation of invincibility.

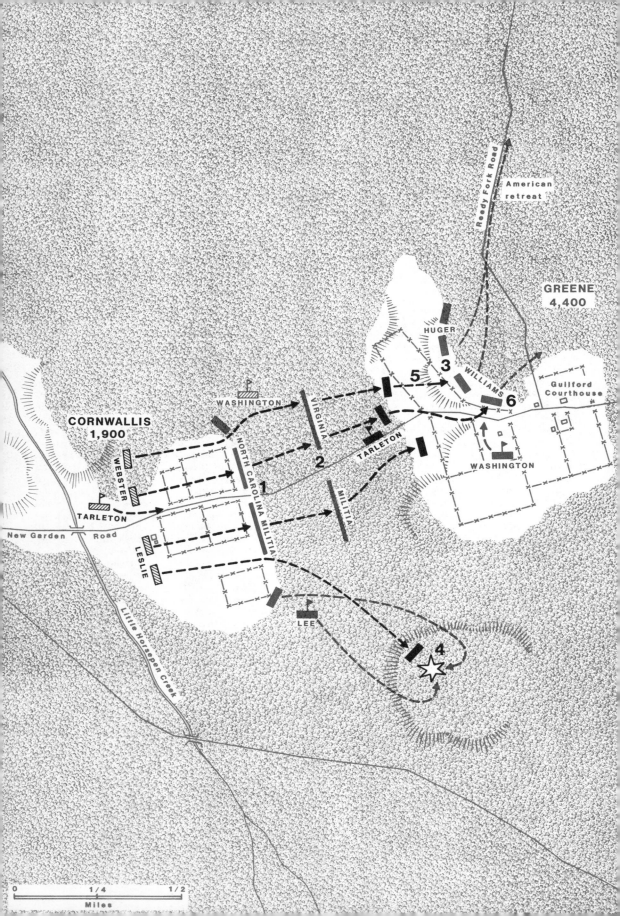

GREENE
4,400

American
retreat

Reedy Fork Road

HUGER

WILLIAMS

Guilford
Courthouse

3

5

6

WASHINGTON

CORNWALLIS
1,900

WASHINGTON

VIRGINIA

NORTH CAROLINA MILITIA

2

TARLETON

WEBSTER

1

MILITIA

TARLETON

New Garden   Road

LESLIE

LEE

4

Little Horsepen Creek

0   1/4   1/2
Miles

MAP # 35

Guilford Court House

March 15, 1781

Despite his victory at Cowpens, Morgan knew that his command remained in a dangerous position. Cornwallis' army lay between Morgan's force and the rest of the American army under Greene. Moreover, the news of Cowpens so infuriated Cornwallis that he immediately started out after Morgan determined to crush the brash Americans and obtain the release of the 525 British prisoners. Following the battle, therefore, Morgan continued his northward retreat. Throughout a rainy, miserable February, Cornwallis's men chased Morgan's small army across North Carolina. So eager was Cornwallis to catch Morgan that he burned his own supply wagons to gain speed, but Morgan stayed always a day's march ahead of him.

The two halves of the American army were reunited at Guilford Courthouse on February 8 and Greene asked his officers if they thought the army should turn and fight. To a man they were opposed. Reluctantly Greene continued the northward retreat. The Americans won a race to the Dan River just over the Virginia border and, lacking boats to follow them across the rain-swollen stream, Cornwallis turned back in disgust to Hillsboro. Greene followed cautiously.

In early March reinforcements of a thousand militia and 550 Continentals raised Greene's total to 4,400, and he decided to seek battle. The American army took a position near Guilford Court House on ground that Greene had reconnoitered earlier, and awaited the British approach. Morgan's ill health had forced his retirement from active service, but Greene borrowed Morgan's tactic of establishing three successive defensive lines. In the first line, behind a rail fence with the woods to their back, Greene placed the untested North Carolina militia (1). From this position the militiamen could fire at the British while they crossed the open fields, now bereft of crops in late-winter. A quarter-mile further east, Greene placed the Virginia militia in heavy woods (2) where the trees would provide cover for the defenders and break up the tight British formations. Another 500 yards further on, Greene placed his 1,400 Continentals atop a slight rise and behind another cleared field (3).

At about one in the afternoon, the British splashed across Little Horsepen Creek and deployed for an attack. The British veterans were already tired when the battle began, having marched twelve miles that morning to reach the battlefield. Nevertheless they made a splendid sight as they advanced across the open corn field in their tight regimental formations. At 150 yards the rail fence in front of them exploded in an uneven volley. Dozens of redcoats fell, but the rest came steadily on and at fifty yards they fired a volley of their own and charged. The North Carolina militia fled into the woods.

The British attackers then entered the thick woods and soon encountered the line of Virginia militia. Here the fighting was fragmented and often hand-to-hand as small groups clashed with one another. The regiment of Hessians pursued the Legion of Light Horse Harry Lee and the riflemen of Colonel William Campbell off to the right and virtually out of the battle (4). The other British regiments encountered fierce resistance especially from Brigadier General Edward Stevens' brigade, but after a half hour they broke through and plunged ahead.

Having fought two battles, the British emerged from the woods to encounter yet another open field and beyond it the 1,400 regulars of the Continental line: Huger's two Virginia regiments on the American right and Williams' two Maryland regiments on the left. Webster's infantry on the British left were the first to emerge from the woods and they charged across the open field and up the slope toward the Continentals (5). A disciplined volley hurled them back into the woods with heavy losses, including Webster, who was mortally wounded. An American victory seemed imminent. But on the other side of the field near the New Garden Road, the British Second Battalion Guards broke the reconstituted Second Maryland Regiment and turned the American left (6). The First Maryland staved off disaster by attacking the Guards in the flank at about the same time that William Washington's cavalry struck them in the rear. To extricate his men, Cornwallis ordered his artillery to fire rounds of grapeshot into the melee. This desperate move killed as many British as Americans but it halted the American counterattack. The outcome of the battle was still in doubt, but the gap in the American line convinced Greene to order a retreat and the Americans gave up the field, abandoning their guns and marching northward up the Reedy Fork Road.

The British attempted a half-hearted pursuit, but they had suffered heavily in the battle and soon gave it up. The Americans had lost 79 killed and 185 wounded, but over 500 British soldiers lay dead or wounded on the field, more than a quarter of Cornwallis' entire command. Cornwallis reported a victory to Germain in enthusiastic terms, but when the Colonial Secretary announced it to Parliament, Opposition leaders scoffed. Charles James Fox remarked dryly that "Another such victory would ruin the British army."

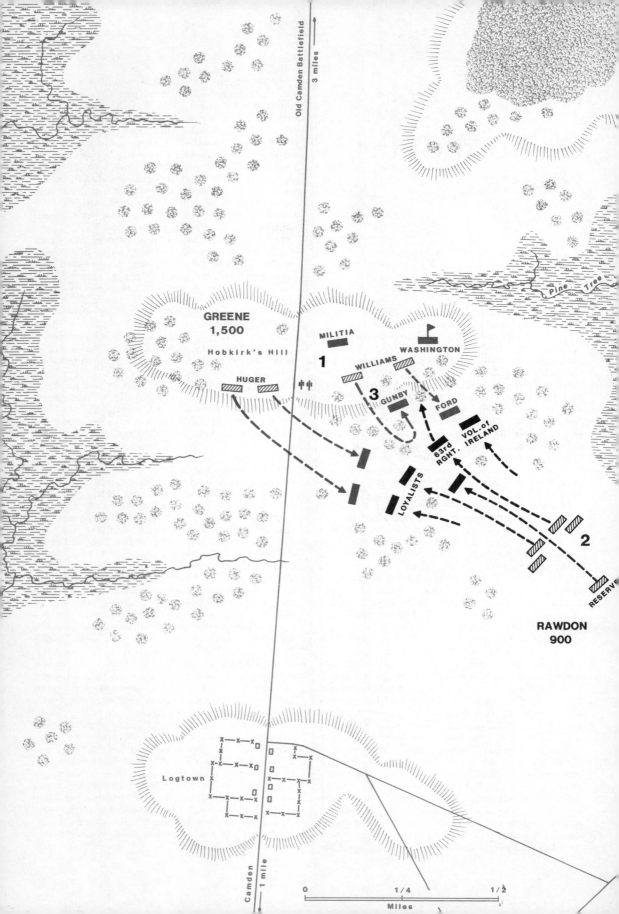

Old Camden Battlefield

← 3 miles

GREENE
1,500

Hobkirk's Hill

MILITIA

WASHINGTON

HUGER

WILLIAMS

1

3

GUNBY

FORD

63rd
RGHT.

VOL. of
IRELAND

LOYALISTS

2

RESERVE

Pine Tree

RAWDON
900

Logtown

Camden ← 1 mile

0   1/4   1/2
Miles

MAP # 36

Hobkirk's Hill

April 25, 1781

Cornwallis rested his army for two days on the bloody ground around Guilford Court House. But his logistic situation dictated that he could neither stay there indefinitely nor pursue Greene. Having burned his wagons when he started out after Morgan in January, Cornwallis now found that the land would not support his army and his supply situation was almost desperate. His men had fought the battle at Guilford Court House without any breakfast and quite literally they did not know where their next meal was coming from. After a two day rest, therefore, Cornwallis ordered his army eastward toward the port city of Wilmington, North Carolina where his men could be supplied by sea. Greene followed him until April 8, then turned southward to reenter South Carolina. Cornwallis let him go. The British commander believed that Rawdon's nearly 8,000 men in South Carolina and Georgia would be capable of dealing with Greene, and Cornwallis had become convinced that final pacification of the Carolinas would become possible only after the conquest of Virginia, where he now focused his attention. Events would prove him wrong on both counts.

Rawdon did indeed command 8,000 men in South Carolina and Georgia, but the figure is misleading for the forces were mostly organized Tory units that were scattered throughout the two states in small garrisons. The largest was at Camden where Rawdon himself commanded 900 men. Greene's strategic plan was to drive the British from these outposts and thereby demonstrate the transience of British control. In the process the British would learn that it is much more difficult to occupy than to conquer.

Greene sent Light Horse Harry Lee's Legion to cooperate with Francis Marion in an attack on Fort Watson — which fell on April 23 — and took his own army in a direct march for Camden. He hoped that Thomas Sumter's forces would join in his attack on Camden, but Sumter never showed up.

Nevertheless, on April 19 Greene's army of some 1,200 Continentals and 250 militia plus William Washington's four score cavalry took up a position on Hobkirk's Hill (1) a mile and a half north of Camden and about three miles south of the battlefield where Gates had come to grief eight months earlier.

Rawdon's family had purchased his commission in the English army while Lord Francis was still a teenager, but Rawdon had proved his military skills on battlefields all over America since the rebellion began in 1775. Still only 26, he did not want to initiate his first independent theatre command with a retreat, so he decided to attack. By arming every man who could carry a weapon (even the musicians according to his report), Rawdon was able to put 900 men in the field. He avoided the main road and approached Greene's camp through the thick woods and on a narrow front in hope of achieving a surprise (2). His leading forces struck the American picket line at about ten a.m. and the American pickets fought well enough to give Greene time to muster and deploy his Continentals.

Assessing the situation, Greene noted the narrow front of the British column and resolved to launch an attack which would overlap both British flanks. But things began to go wrong almost at once. Rawdon was quick to bring up his second line and extend his flanks to counter Greene's maneuver, and, more critically, the First Maryland regiment that had behaved so well at Guilford Court House, fell into confusion. Captain William Beatty commanding its right-hand company was shot down early in the attack and his men halted in confusion. This broke the front of the regiment and rather than hurry the laggards forward, the regimental commander, Colonel John Gunby, halted the whole line and ordered the regiment back to the base of the hill to reform (3). This move exposed the flanks of the regiments on either side and the American advance faltered. Greene had to order a general withdrawal.

The Americans fell back three miles to the old Camden battlefield and Rawdon's men were left in command of the hill. They did not stay there, however; instead Rawdon withdrew into his fortifications around Camden. Indeed, despite 500 British reinforcements that arrived on May 7 Rawdon decided that he had to abandon his exposed position at Camden and on May 10 he began a slow withdrawal toward Charleston.

Though in itself indecisive, the battle of Hobkirk's Hill marked the beginning of a general British withdrawal from the interior of South Carolina. In the ensuing five weeks, Marion, Pickens, and Lee captured a half dozen British posts including Augusta which fell on June 5. Only Fort Ninety Six held out against an American siege when Rawdon brought up a relief column from Charleston that included three fresh regiments from England. Soon afterward, however, the British evacuated even this post and by August they only held Savannah and Charleston. After a year and a half of campaigning, the British were back where they had started.

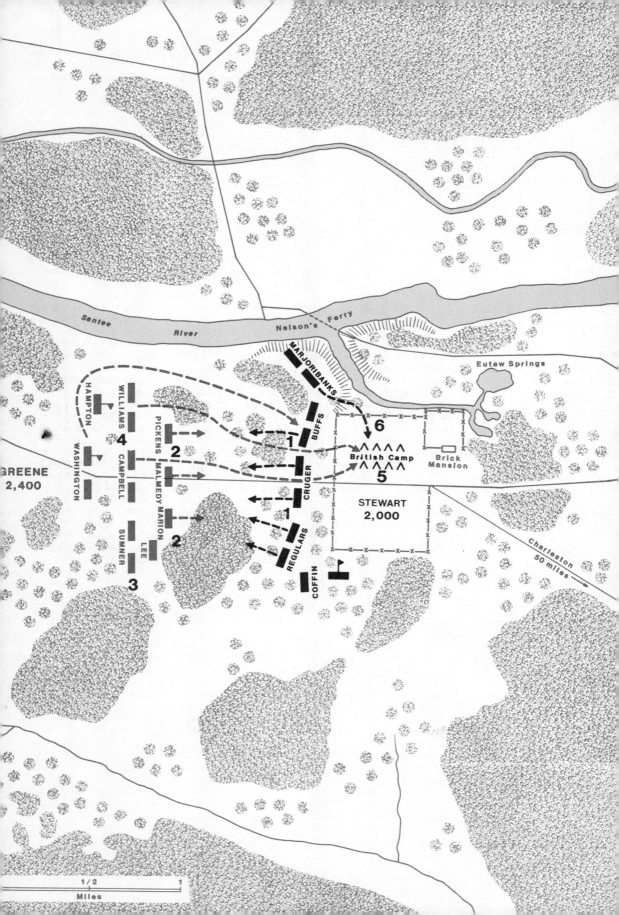

Eutaw Springs

Nelson's Ferry

Santee River

MARJORIBANKS

BUFFS

CRUGER

REGULARS

COFFIN

HAMPTON

WILLIAMS

PICKENS

WASHINGTON

CAMPBELL

MALMEDY MARION

SUMNER

LEE

GREENE
2,400

British Camp

Brick
Mansion

STEWART
2,000

Charleston
50 miles

1

2

4

2

1

2

3

5

6

1/2   1
Miles

MAP # 37

Eutaw Springs

September 8, 1781

The long summer campaign in South Carolina ruined Lord Rawdon's health as well as his spirit. After his futile chase of Greene following the siege of Ninety Six, Rawdon turned his command over to Lieutenant Colonel Alexander Stewart of the British Third Regiment — the Irish Buffs — and sailed for England. Alas for both his health and his spirit, his ship was captured en route by de Grasse's fleet and Rawdon became an unwilling and unhappy witness to the Battle of the Virginia Capes (see MAP # 40) from the deck of a French warship. For his part, Stewart established his camp at Eutaw Springs on the south bank of the Santee about fifty miles northwest of Charleston, content to leave the initiative to the rebels.

The Americans had also suffered from the heat of a midsummer campaign in the miasmatic air of the Carolina Piedmont. After the siege of Ninety Six, therefore, Greene took his army to the more comfortable and healthful High Hills of Santee on the east bank of the Wateree south of Camden (see MAP # 31). On these sandy hills 200 feet above the swampy lowlands, the Americans rested for six weeks. Then on August 22 Greene moved his army north to Camden, crossed the Wateree, and turned south heading for Stewart's camp at Eutaw Springs.

About half of Greene's army of 2,400 were Continentals. Stewart's force was a little smaller, but a large majority of his men were regulars. In addition to his own regiment, he had the 63rd and 64th as well as Colonel John Cruger's garrison excavated from Ninety Six — a total of about 2,000 men. One leading authority has postulated that in no other battle of the war were the opposing sides so nearly equal in strength. But Greene

had one very clear advantage: knowledge of the enemy's whereabouts. It was clear evidence of the decline of loyalist sympathy in South Carolina that Greene's army could approach to within four miles of Stewart's camp without the British commander being informed of it by friendly citizens. As it was, Stewart learned of the Americans' approach only when a party of men sent out to harvest yams for the army's rations ran headlong into Greene's front line. The American militia sent them fleeing, but the accidental meeting gave Stewart a chance to deploy his men a hundred yards or so west of his camp (1).

As in his earlier battles, Greene placed his militia in the front line (2) hoping they would take the starch out of the British before he sent in his Continentals. Indeed, the militiamen fought very well this day, exchanging several volleys with the British regulars and loyalists toe-to-toe before they finally gave way to a British bayonet charge. When they did break, Greene sent forward Major General Jethro Sumner's three brigades of North Carolina Continentals (3). They reestablished the American line, and the battle continued until they, too, were finally broken by a British bayonet attack. But Greene still had his best troops left: the Maryland and Virginia veterans of Guilford Court House and Hobkirk's Hill (4). They met the British head on and drove them back all the way to their camp and beyond it. The chance for a decisive victory was thrown away when the Americans caught sight of the abandoned British camp (5). Row upon row of canvas tents, boxes of supplies, food, and even spirits lay there for the taking. The Americans stopped their headlong pursuit and began to loot the camp.

The halt gave Major John Marjoribanks his opportunity. Having already inflicted heavy casualties on the cavalry (including wounding and capturing William Washington himself), Majoribanks now marched his men to the cover of the brick mansion just beyond the British camp and from his new position he drove off the American looters (6). His units now completely disorganized, Greene broke off the fight and withdrew.

The British held the field, but they had come very close to complete disaster. Both sides suffered heavy losses. Stewart lost 85 killed, 351 wounded, and another 257 listed as missing — probably deserted. The Americans lost 138 killed, 375 wounded, and 41 missing. Nevertheless, in the same pattern as earlier British "victories" in the South, Stewart determined soon afterward that despite his escape, he would withdraw to safer ground, in this case to Charleston.

The Battle of Eutaw Springs was the last clash between British and American soldiers in the South. Though the civil war between Loyalists and Whigs continued into 1782, the British did not again venture out of their strongholds in Charleston and Savannah. With Clinton apparently willing to remain passive in New York, Cornwallis commanded the last active British field army in America, but even as Stewart withdrew his army to Charleston, events were moving to a climax in Virginia.

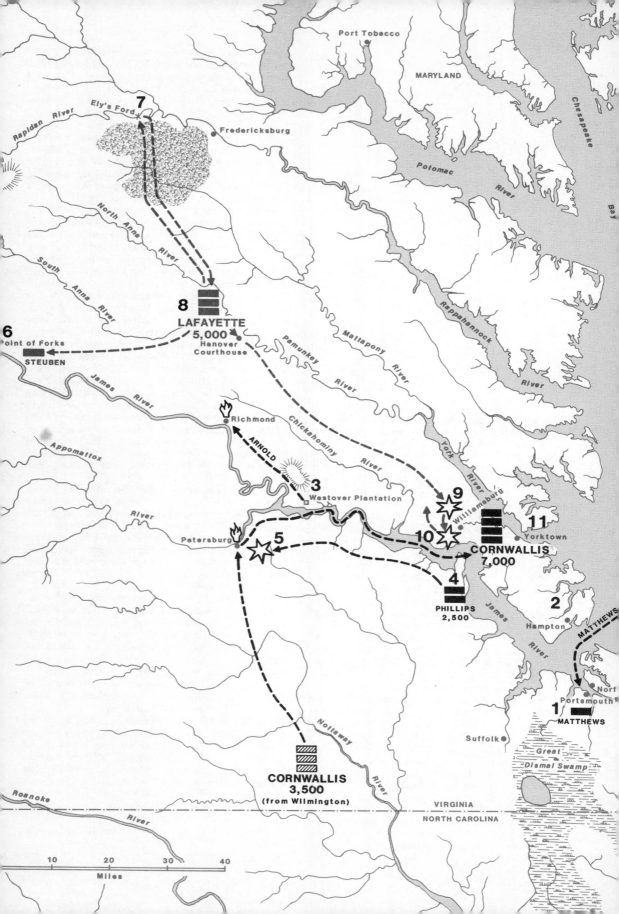

Port Tobacco

MARYLAND

Rapidan River

Ely's Ford **7**

Fredericksburg

Potomac River

Chesapeake Bay

North Anna River

South Anna River

6
Point of Forks
STEUBEN

8
LAFAYETTE
5,000
Hanover Courthouse

Pamunkey River

Mattapony River

Rappahannock River

James River

Appomattox River

Richmond

ARNOLD

Chickahominy River

Westover Plantation **3**

York River

9
Williamsburg

11
CORNWALLIS
7,000
Yorktown

Petersburg

5

10

4
PHILLIPS
2,500

2

Hampton

MATTHEWS

James River

Norf
Portsmouth

1
MATTHEWS

Suffolk

Great
Dismal Swamp

Nottaway River

CORNWALLIS
3,500
(from Wilmington)

Roanoke River

VIRGINIA
NORTH CAROLINA

10   20   30   40
Miles

MAP # 38

Cornwallis vs. Lafayette

Summer, 1781

His experience in the Carolinas confirmed Cornwallis in his opinion that Virginia was the keystone to the rebellion. Not only was it the largest colony, and one of the richest, but its central location meant that all supplies and communications between Washington's army on the Hudson and Greene's southern army had to pass through its territory. Moreover, the Chesapeake Bay and the several rivers that flowed into it provided avenues of invasion for a water-borne army. As early as the Spring of 1779, therefore, Cornwallis began urging Clinton to send an expedition from New York to secure Virginia. And, after resting briefly at Wilmington following his contest with Greene at Guilford Court House, Cornwallis determined to take his own army there as well.

Though he was more dubious about the strategic importance of Virginia, Clinton complied with Cornwallis' request and in May 1779 he sent 1,800 men under Major General Edward Matthews to Portsmouth (1). Matthews' force encountered no real opposition and easily occupied not only Portsmouth, but also Norfolk and Suffolk. The British invaders made no friends for the crown by their behavior. They burned barns, crops, and homes almost indiscriminately. In 1781 Benedict Arnold, now a British Brigadier General, led another raid into Virginia. He arrived at Hampton Roads (2) on December 30, 1780, sailed up the James River to Westover (3), and marched to Richmond. After burning much of the city, he returned to Portsmouth. In response to these raids, and expecially eager to capture Arnold if possible, Washington dispatched 1,200 men under Major General the Marquis de Lafayette to Virginia.

Lafayette's small army arrived in Virginia in mid-March. The original plan called for Lafayette's force to cooperate with a French squadron from Newport, but when the French ships arrived in the Chesapeake Bay, they found a large British squadron already there and they returned to New-

port. Even more seriously Clinton sent another British army of 2,600 men to Virginia under Major General William Phillips (4). Phillip's army advanced up the James River, drove off 1,000 Virginia militia outside Petersburg (5), and looted the city.

Lafayette reached Richmond on April 29 in time to prevent Phillips from burning that city too, but on May 20 Cornwallis arrived in Petersburg at the end of his long march from Wilmington. "It now appears that I have business with two armies," Lafayette wrote to Washington. Indeed the strength of the combined British armies in Virginia now topped 7,000 and presented Lafayette with a delicate problem. If he fought a battle he would almost surely be destroyed, but if he avoided the enemy altogether he would lose the allegiance and confidence of the Virginia militia on which he depended. He therefore adopted a middle course. "I am determined to skirmish," he wrote, "but not to engage too far." Lafayette sent General von Steuben west to Point of Forks (6) with the army's supplies and retreated northward with the rest of his army to Ely's Ford on the Rapidan (7). Having despaired of catching up to Lafayette, Cornwallis sent Tarleton's dragoons on a flying raid to Charlottesville (not shown), where they nearly captured Governor Thomas Jefferson.

On June 10 Anthony Wayne's brigade of Pennsylvanians joined Lafayette's army in its new camp on the South Anna River (8) and a few days later William Campbell's 600 riflemen also came into camp. Lafayette now commanded nearly 5,000 men, including militia, and he advanced cautiously southward. On June 26 elements of the two armies fought a sharp skirmish just west of Cornwallis' camp at Williamsburg (9).

Meanwhile the threat of an imminent junction between Rochambeau's 4,000 men in Newport and Washington's army outside New York convinced Clinton that he was about to be attacked. He therefore ordered Cornwallis to return 3,000 of his troops from Virginia to New York. In order to comply, Cornwallis left Williamsburg on July 4 to cross the James River en route to Portsmouth where the troops could be embarked. Lafayette determined to strike Cornwallis while the British army was astride the James. On July 6 he sent 500 men under Anthony Wayne against what he believed was Cornwallis' rear guard at Greenspring (10). But in fact Cornwallis had sent his baggage across the river first, and his entire army was still on the northern bank. When Wayne's men attacked they found themselves in serious danger of being annihilated. Wayne ordered a desperation bayonet attack to extricate his force from the British and, though he did manage to escape with the bulk of his forces, his unit was badly mauled. Cornwallis proceeded to Portsmouth with his army, but Clinton had already countermanded the order to send reinforcements and he now directed Cornwallis to occupy and hold a deep water seaport for the British fleet. Obediently, Cornwallis shipped his army to Yorktown (11), and Lafayette occupied Williamsburg.

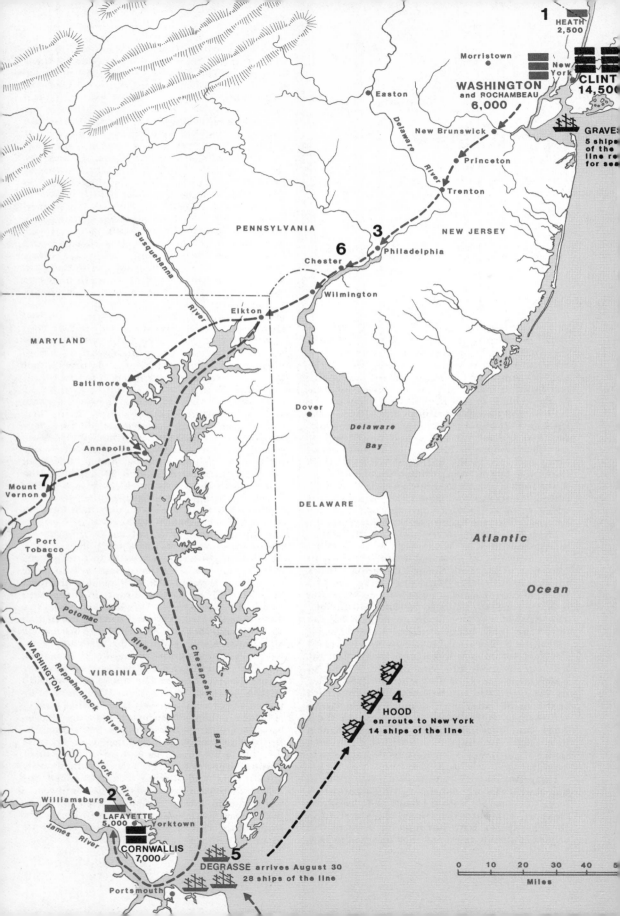

1 HEATH
2,500

Morristown

Easton

New York

CLINT
14,500

WASHINGTON
and ROCHAMBEAU
6,000

New Brunswick

GRAVE:
5 ships
of the
line re
for sea

Princeton

Trenton

PENNSYLVANIA

NEW JERSEY

3

Philadelphia

6

Chester

Wilmington

Elkton

Susquehanna River

MARYLAND

Baltimore

Dover

Delaware
Bay

Annapolis

7

Mount
Vernon

DELAWARE

Atlantic

Port
Tobacco

Ocean

Potomac

Rappahannock River

VIRGINIA

River

Chesapeake Bay

WASHINGTON

4

HOOD
en route to New York
14 ships of the line

Williamsburg

2

LAFAYETTE
5,000

York River

Yorktown

James River

CORNWALLIS
7,000

Portsmouth

5

DEGRASSE arrives August 30
28 ships of the line

0   10   20   30   40   5
Miles

MAP # 39

March to the Chesapeake

August-September, 1781

Throughout the campaign seasons of 1779 and 1780, the American army under George Washington languished in and around its camp in the Hudson River highlands. For nearly two years Washington had husbanded his forces in an effort to maintain the fiction that his ragged force of 3,500 was besieging Clinton's army of 14,500 spit-and-polish veterans on Manhattan Island. All this while, the national attitude toward the war effort and the army could best be described as apathetic. The men had no real uniforms, poor rations, and they had not been paid in months. When they were paid it was in Continental scrip which was virtually worthless and spawned the phrase "not worth a Continental." In April 1781 Washington wrote plaintively to Congress: "We are at the end of our tether."

Then on May 22 Washington learned that Admiral de Grasse planned to bring his French fleet from the Caribbean to American waters in the fall. Notwithstanding the precarious condition of his army, the news of de Grasse's intentions reawakened long-held plans of wresting New York away from the British. In June Washington discussed the prospects of a combined attack on New York with Count Jean-Baptiste de Rochambeau, commander of the French garrison of 4,000 men at Newport. Rochambeau was dubious about the practicability of attacking New York, but he deferred to Washington and in the first week of July he started his men marching southward from Newport. Washington called up the local militia and by the end of July the allies had assembled an army of over 9,000 men — half American and half French — on the Hudson.

Throughout July and early August Washington and Rochambeau reconnoitered the shores of Manhattan Island looking for a weak spot in the British defenses. Finally and reluctantly Washington agreed that there was no weak spot. Rochambeau, meanwhile, had written to de Grasse suggesting the Chesapeake as a possible theatre for a combined operation and on August 14 Washington received a letter from de Grasse in which the French admiral announced that he was sailing for the Chesapeake Bay, that he would arrive sometime that month, and that he could stay only until mid-October. So committed was Washington to the idea of an attack on New York that he was initially disappointed by the news, but he soon accepted the situation and adjusted his plans accordingly. He would leave Major General William Heath with 2,500 men on the Hudson (1) to watch Clinton, and take the rest of the army (2,000 Americans and 4,000 French) overland to join Lafayette on the Yorktown penninsula (2). There was a substantial risk involved. If Clinton discovered the plan, he could sortie from the city and overwhelm Heath or even catch the allied army on the march and destroy it. Great secrecy was therefore maintained and a planned campaign of deception built into the operation. False orders were written and allowed to fall into enemy hands; bread-baking ovens were built in northern New Jersey to create the appearance of a permanent bivouac for the French.

The allied army began its march south on August 21 with Clinton still completely in the dark. So certain was he that New York was the object of the Franco-American maneuver, that he continued to insist that the southward movement was a feint until September 2 when he wrote Cornwallis that it appeared the American army was headed south. On that day Washington's soldiers were parading through Philadelphia (3).

Stealing a march on Clinton was important, but the campaign would be for naught without de Grasse and the French fleet. De Grasse had left Cap François with 28 ships of the line on August 5. Admiral Sir Samuel Hood, commanding the British Caribbean squadron at Antigua, had only 14 ships of the line but he assumed that only a part of the French fleet was en route to America and so he set out in pursuit. But where were the French headed? There were only two possibilities: the Chesapeake or New York. Hood sped to the Chesapeake first, arriving on August 25. He looked into the Bay but saw no sign of de Grasse and so he sailed on to New York (4). In fact, de Grasse had stopped at Havana on his way to the Chesapeake and was therefore five full days behind. On August 30 the French fleet dropped anchor unmolested in Chesapeake Bay (5).

When Washington learned of de Grasse's arrival in the Chesapeake he was transformed. As Rochambeau was arriving at Chester (6), he was perplexed to see the normally taciturn and dignified General Washington dancing around on the dock and waving his hat. His confusion turned to amazement when he stepped ashore and Washington grabbed him in a bear hug and whirled him around the pier. He had good cause for joy. De Grasse had brought 2,500 French soldiers with him, and these forces, joined with Lafayette's army, were enough to hold Cornwallis in place until the main allied army arrived. Cornwallis was trapped! After a flying visit to Mount Vernon (7), his first since the war began, Washington hurried on to Williamsburg for a decisive confrontation with Cornwallis.

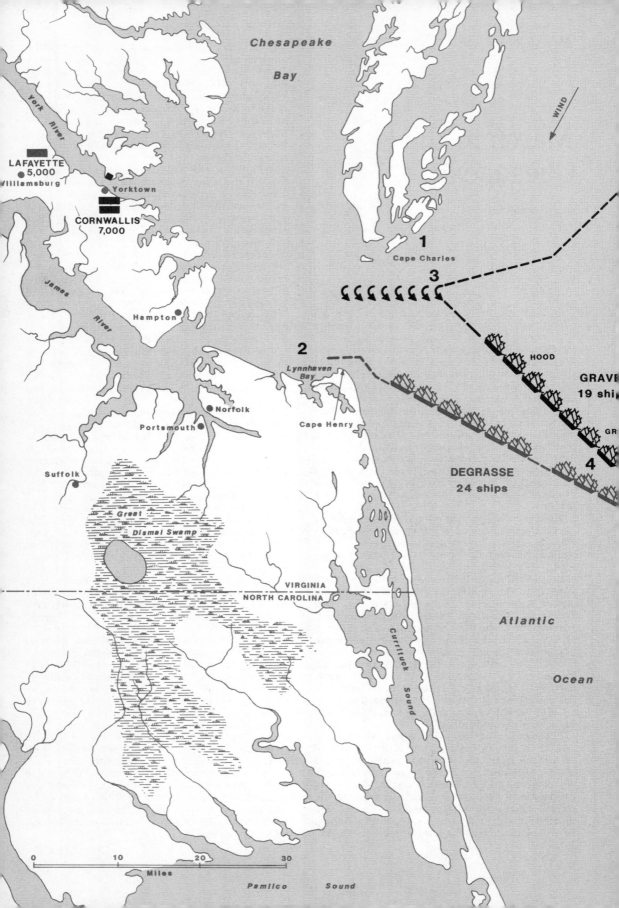

Chesapeake

Bay

WIND

York River

LAFAYETTE
● 5,000
Williamsburg

Yorktown

CORNWALLIS
7,000

1

Cape Charles

3

HOOD

GRAVE
19 ship

James River

Hampton

2

Lynnhaven Bay

Cape Henry

GR

4

DEGRASSE
24 ships

Norfolk

Portsmouth

Suffolk

Great
Dismal Swamp

VIRGINIA
NORTH CAROLINA

Currituck Sound

Atlantic

Ocean

0   10   20   30
Miles

Pamlico   Sound

MAP # 40

Battle of the Virginia Capes

September 5, 1781

After looking into Chesapeake Bay on August 25, Admiral Hood had continued on to New York where he informed Admiral Samuel Graves of de Grasse's departure from the Caribbean. As the senior naval officer, Graves now had to decide what to do. It was not yet clear to either Graves or Clinton that it was Cornwallis at Yorktown and not New York that was the target of all this maneuvering. But the aggressive Hood was anxious to return to the Chesapeake and he urged his superior to put to sea. Graves would not be rushed. He had several ships in need of repair and not until September 1 did he bring five of his vessels over the bar at Sandy Hook. The combined British fleet numbered nineteen ships of the line, still significantly weaker than de Grasse's fleet. Ignorant of the strength or location of the phantom French fleet, Graves and Hood headed south to find the enemy.

The British arrived off Cape Charles (1) at dawn on September 5 and spied the bare masts of a large fleet just inside the capes in Lynnhaven Bay (2). Though unable to determine the exact strength of this fleet, the British nevertheless headed for the entrance to the Bay, running before the northeast breeze on the starboard tack.

De Grasse might have remained in the bay and awaited the British challenge there, but he knew that Admiral de Barras' squadron from Newport was on its way to the Chesapeake with Rochambeau's siege artillery and he could not allow this British fleet to intercept it. He could do nothing, however, until the tide turned. All morning he and his staff watched and counted the approaching topsails, and then at noon when the tide turned, de Grasse ordered his ships to slip their cables, make for the entrance, and form line of battle.

Two hours later, with the French vessels straggling out past Cape Henry, Graves ordered the British fleet to come about on the port tack (3), thus reversing the order of the vessels in the battle line. Hood, who had commanded the van division, now occupied the rear. Hood assumed that Graves would immediately order the British fleet to bear down on the French, still only par-

tially formed, their first five vessels a good mile ahead of the rest of the fleet. But for a full hour Graves was content to plow through the green Atlantic swells on a parallel course and allow de Grasse time to close up his battle line. Already impatient at his superior's timorousness, Hood was both perplexed and angered by this decision. Finally at three p.m. Graves hoisted the signal for action, but he continued to fly the signal for a line ahead formation.

For nearly a century the British permanent fighting instructions had dictated that the ships of a British battle fleet should remain in a strict line ahead formation until the enemy's line had been broken. Only then could individual ship captains attempt to break through the enemy line or double up on enemy ships. Such tactics minimized the possibility of a disastrous defeat, but also made a decisive victory unlikely. A few young officers had recently criticized the permanent fighting instruction, claiming that there were circumstances when breaking with convention could catch the enemy off guard and produce a spectacular victory. Advocates of this school of thought might have argued that the circumstances facing Graves and Hood on September 5, 1781 were a case in point. The French had superior numbers and an even greater superiority in weight of broadside. Even given the tradition of British naval superiority, it was unlikely that conservative tactics could break through de Grasse's fleet and succor Cornwallis.

As the two fleets closed with one another at about a thirty degree angle, only the lead vessels came within range (4). Under the circumstances Hood might have taken his ships out of the line to swoop down on the French center, but Graves continued to fly the line ahead signal and such a bold action would have violated the permanent fighting instructions. Though a Horatio Nelson or even a John Paul Jones might have turned a blind eye to the signal. Hood held his position in line and as a result his ships remained out of the battle altogether until 5:30 when Graves finally hauled down the line ahead signal. But a half hour later the two fleets drew apart and the battle was over. Only eight British and fifteen French vessels had been heavily engaged in the two hour battle.

The lead vessels of both fleets suffered serious damage, but the British suffered more because of the superior French weight of broadside. The only vessel lost in the battle was the British 74 gun *Thunderer* which sank two days later. For five days the two fleets maneuvered within sight of one another though they did not renew the action. On September 10 de Grasse returned to the Chesapeake and discovered that de Barras's squadron had slipped into the Bay. The combined French fleet now numbered 35 ships of the line and, giving it up as a lost cause, Graves returned to New York. Tactically indecisive, the Battle of the Virginia Capes was nevertheless the most strategically significant naval battle of the war. It confirmed French command of the Chesapeake and sealed the fate of Cornwallis' army.

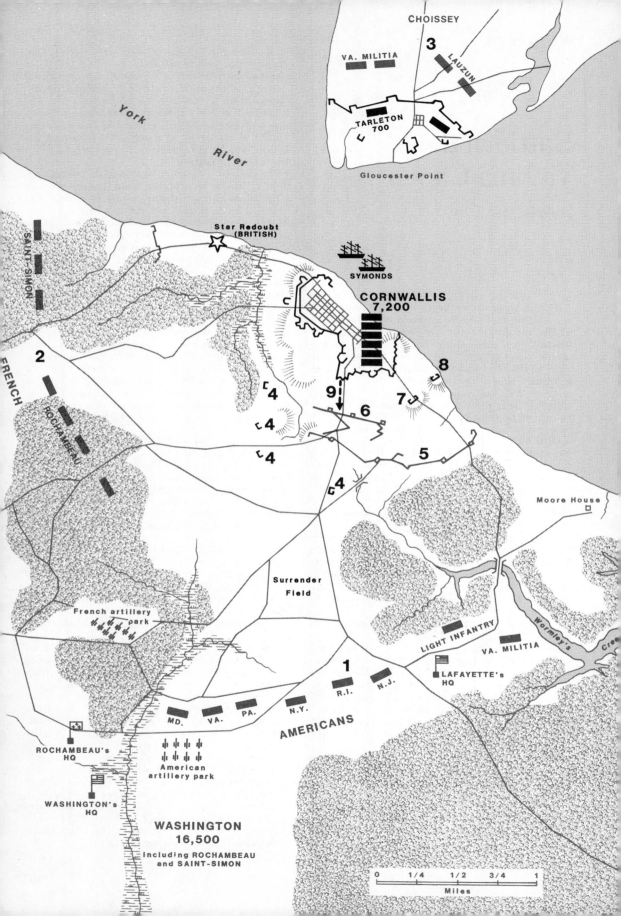

CHOISSEY

3

VA. MILITIA

LAUZUN

TARLETON
700

Gloucester Point

York

River

SAINT-SIMON

Star Redoubt
(BRITISH)

SYMONDS

CORNWALLIS
7,200

FRENCH

2

ROCHAMBEAU

4

4

4

9

6

7

8

5

4

Moore House

Surrender
Field

French artillery
park

LIGHT INFANTRY

VA. MILITIA

LAFAYETTE's
HQ

Wormley's

Creek

1

R.I.

N.J.

MD.

VA.

PA.

N.Y.

AMERICANS

ROCHAMBEAU's
HQ

American
artillery park

WASHINGTON's
HQ

WASHINGTON
16,500

including ROCHAMBEAU
and SAINT-SIMON

0   1/4   1/2   3/4   1
Miles

MAP # 41

The Siege of Yorktown

September - October, 1781

Washington and Rochambeau arrived in Lafayette's camp at Williamsburg on September 14 after the flying trip to Mount Vernon. The allied army was still strung out behind them for hundreds of miles and the last of the soldiers would not arrive for another ten days. But the addition of the troops brought by de Grasse gave Lafayette an army of 8,500 — larger than the British army at Yorktown — and Washington was confident that Lafayette's men could hold Cornwallis on the peninsula until the rest of the army arrived. The only question in his mind involved de Grasse. Washington knew that an allied siege of Yorktown could be brought to a successful conclusion only if the French fleet remained in the Chesapeake. With that concern uppermost in his mind, Washington boarded a small cutter on the James River on September 17 and sailed out into Hampton Roads to visit de Grasse in his flagship, the giant three-deck *Ville de Paris*. The meeting was cordial (de Grasse kissed Washington on both cheeks and called him "my dear little General") and the French admiral agreed to keep his fleet in the Chesapeake at least until the end of the month. Satisfied, Washington climbed back into the cutter for the return to Williamsburg, though frustrating offshore winds kept him literally at sea until September 22.

With de Grasse's agreement to remain in the Bay and the arrival of the last of the soldiers from New York, the allied grand army marched out of Williamsburg for Yorktown at 5 a.m. on September 28. The Americans established their camp south and east of the city (1), and the French set up to the west (2). In addition Washington sent a substantial force under the Comte de Choissey across the York River to watch the 700 men that Cornwallis had posted at Gloucester Point (3).

For his part Cornwallis had recently received a letter from Clinton promising to send a relief force of 5,000 men, and rather than challenge the advancing allied army, he instead gave up all his outer works (4) and retreated within his fortifications around the city. This decision was criticized then and since on the grounds that Cornwallis gave up what it would otherwise have taken the allies weeks to capture by regular siege methods.

Over the next two weeks the allies tightened the noose about Yorktown. On the night of October 6 the French and Americans began the construction of the first parallel of formal siege operations (5). Fifteen hundred men wielded picks and shovels and by dawn a trench 2,000 yards long faced the British southwest salient. Two days later the allied heavy guns opened fire on the British works and kept up the bombardment all night. The physical damage to Yorktown was extensive, but the steady loss of life and the constant psychological pressure was worse. On October 10 after an all-night bombardment Cornwallis wrote to Clinton: "nothing but a direct move to the York River which includes a successful naval action can save us." Ominously he added: "we cannot hope to make a very long resistance." Smallpox had broken out in the city.

On the night of October 11, Washington's men began work on a second parallel (6), but two British redoubts had to be taken before the line could be extended to the river. On the night of October 14, therefore, the allies assaulted these redoubts. The French under General Count William Deux-Ponts assaulted Redoubt # 9 (7) and the Americans, commanded by Colonel Alexander Hamilton, stormed # 10 (8). The well-planned attacks achieved complete success and that same night the American sappers began extending the second parallel to include the new strong points. The allies were now only 250 yards from the British lines. The next morning Cornwallis wrote Clinton: "My situation now becomes very critical."

Cornwallis's younger officers chafed at their commander's inactivity. They urged him to mount a sortie or attempt a breakout. He complied half-heartedly. Just before dawn on October 16, Lieutenant Colonel Robert Abercrombie led a sortie of 350 men against the allied lines. They took some prisoners and spiked six guns (9), but such efforts could only delay the inevitable unless the British army broke out of its encirclement. That night, therefore, Cornwallis sent his wounded and 1,000 Guards and light infantry across the river to Gloucester Point, planning to break out to the north and march overland to New York. But when the boats attempted to return for a second trip, a furious storm scattered them all over the river. Cornwallis gave it up. Out of artillery shells, his works all but destroyed, and his spirit broken, he decided to negotiate.

At 9 a.m. on October 17, a red-coated drummer boy appeared atop the British parapet and began to beat the long roll. Gradually the allied guns fell silent and a British lieutenant appeared on the rampart holding a white handkerchief high over his head. Silently the men of both armies watched his march across the shell-torn no man's land. There wasn't a man in either army that didn't know what it meant.

Epilogue: The World Turned Upside Down

Negotiations between the two armies at Yorktown took place in the Moore House a half mile behind the American lines. Cornwallis attempted to obtain the kind of terms that Burgoyne had received from Gates at Saratoga: the British soldiers would return to England (and the Germans to Germany) giving their parole not to fight again in the war unless exchanged. But Washington would not hear of it. The army was to be surrendered and taken to camps of confinement. Moreover, the American negotiators insisted on the same terms of surrender that Cornwallis had demanded of Lincoln at Charleston: the British would march out of their fortifications around Yorktown with their flags furled and playing one of their own tunes. One of the conventions of eighteenth century warfare was that the surrendering army played one of the enemy's tunes as a final gesture of defiance. But Cornwallis had disallowed this gesture at Charleston, and Colonel John Laurens, who had been with Lincoln at Charleston, remembered. When the British objected to the harshness of the requirement, Laurens proclaimed "This remains an article, or I cease to be a commissioner." In fact, a specific reference to the terms at "Charles Town" was written into the surrender document. Cornwallis would have to pay the final humiliation.

At eleven o'clock in the morning of October 19, Washington, Rochambeau, and Admiral de Barras (representing de Grasse) met at Redoubt # 10. A messenger delivered the signed surrender document (Cornwallis signed for the army and Captain Thomas Symonds for the Royal Navy). The allied commanders signed, and it was done. An hour later the French and American armies lined up

American Major General Benjamin Lincoln (mounted in center) accepts the British surrender at Yorktown from General O'Hara. Lord Cornwallis avoided the ceremony pleading ill health. Washington is the mounted figure on the right in this painting by John Trumbull. (NA)

facing each other in parallel lines on the surrender field. They waited more than two hours for the British, but the mood was light rather than tense, and bands of both armies entertained one another with popular songs. Finally at about 2 p.m. the British appeared. An impeccably dressed officer rode at the head of the long red column as it wound its way out of the city and passed between the lines of French and Americans. The music they marched to was a popular London song of the season, a completely unmilitary tune whose name was "The World Turned Upside Down." Selected because the British did not want to sully one of their own military marches at this humiliation, its title was wholly appropriate. The British soldiers were not at their best. They marched out of step and allowed their eyes to wander to the ranks of their enemies. They were impressed by the French, but more astonished by the ragged and unmilitary-looking Americans.

The man who led them was not Cornwallis, but Brigadier General Charles O'Hara. O'Hara sat erect in his saddle and rode directly to Count Rochambeau at the head of the French troops. Clearly it was his intent to offer surrender to the Frenchman. But Rochambeau shook his head. "We are subordinate to the Americans," he told O'Hara in French, and gestured to General Washington astride his gray sorrel. Dutifully O'Hara rode to face Washington. He offered an apology for the absence of Cornwallis who, O'Hara explained, was sick. (Sick at heart, thought many of those within hearing.) If he was disappointed, Washington did not show it. He directed O'Hara to receive his instructions from General Lincoln, his own second in command. It was a sweet moment for Lincoln who had been on the other side of a similar ceremony only a year earlier.

One by one the once proud but now sullen British regiments passed through the gauntlet into an enclosed space, grounded arms, and then marched back out. A few companies hurled their weapons with fury onto the growing pile of arms,

Washington resigns his Commission at Annapolis on December 23, 1783 (U.S. Capitol)

but a sharp word from Lincoln forced them to lay down their arms more gently. The demeanor of the British officers was more stoic. That night officers on both sides hosted dinner parties and there were songs and jokes all around. Such parties became so obligatory that General von Steuben felt obliged to borrow money to host a party of this own; he felt that otherwise his honor would be sullied.

The surrender of Yorktown did not end the war. King George saw it as merely another setback, and was ready to continue. But news of the disaster shook the North ministry to its very foundations. More politically astute than his sovereign, Lord North recognized at once the impact that Yorktown would have on the Commons. "Oh God!" he cried when he heard the news. "It is all over!" Not quite. His ministry staggered on for another five months until in March of 1782 he was forced to resign, his place taken by Lord Rockingham. The king was despondent. "I do not abandon you," he told North. "It is you who abandon me." But North had no choice; there was simply no support for a continuation of the war in the House of Commons. Under Rockingham, negotiations for a comprehensive peace were undertaken at once though a final document was not signed in Paris until September 3, 1783.

The war sputtered on while the negotiators talked. In particular British and French fleets contested for dominance in the Lesser Antilles. In the Battle of the Saints in April, 1782 the British fleet of Admiral George Rodney mauled the French fleet and actually captured de Grasse. Concerned

now that the American insistence on a preliminary British recognition of American independence would prolong the expensive war indefinitely, the French began to negotiate separately and the Americans feared abandonment by their ally. Franklin, therefore, opened up separate negotiations of his own and all the powers engaged in diplomatic maneuverings that, however delicate, were ultimately successful. In November, British and American representatives initialed a draft agreement, the first article of which read: "His Britannic Majesty acknowledges the said United States . . . to be free, sovereign, and independent." The following January preliminary articles were accepted by all the parties and military operations ceased. Finally in September, after a year and a half of negotiations, the Peace of Paris was signed and the war ended.

There were many heroes in the war, and not a few villains. But the American victory, so improbable in 1776, was more than anything else the personal achievement of General George Washington. Whatever may be said of Saratoga as the turning point, or the decisive importance of French assistance, it was the determination, patience, and character of George Washington that made final victory possible. He held the army together when the cause was darkest; he declined dictatorship when it could have been his for the asking; he treated Congress with respect even when its actions and pronouncements merited only scorn. A true hero of the Revolution, Washington rode home to Mount Vernon in the fall of 1783 happy to lay down his burden.

Suggestions for Further Reading

The following list is not intended as a bibliography, but rather as a list of secondary narrative accounts in which the battles of the American Revolution are described in greater detail than was possible here. There are, in addition, a number of general works on the military aspects of the American Revolution. By far the most useful and authoritative is Christopher Ward's two-volume history entitled *The War of the Revolution* (New York, 1952). It is both informative and entertaining. In addition the inaugural volume (Volume II) in the Oxford History of the United States, *The Glorious Cause: The American Revolution, 1763-1789* (New York, 1982), covers the social and political aspects of the war as well as the military campaigns. See also Don Higginbotham, *The War of American Independence* (Boston, 1971, 1983) and Willard M. Wallace, *Appeal to Arms: A Military History of the American Revolution* (New York, 1951). A much older book, more exclusively military in its orientation but not altogether as reliable is Colonel Henry B. Carrington, *Battles of the American Revolution, 1775-1781* (New York, 1876). In addition the masterful biographies of George Washington by Douglas Southall Freeman and James Flexner are essential reading.

MAPS 1-2: LEXINGTON AND CONCORD

Arthur B. Tourtellot, *Lexington and Concord* (New York, 1959)
Originally published as *William Diamond's Drum*

MAP 3: THE SIEGE OF BOSTON

Donald B. Chidsey, *The Siege of Boston* (New York, 1966)
Richard Frothingham, *History of the Siege of Boston and the Battles of Lexington, Concord and Bunker Hill* (New York, 1970)

MAP 4: BUNKER HILL

Thomas J. Fleming, *Now We are Enemies: The Story of Bunker Hill* (New York, 1960)
Richard M. Ketchum, *The Battle for Bunker Hill* (New York, 1962)

MAPS 5-7: THE AMERICAN INVASION OF CANADA

Harrison Bird, *Attack on Quebec: The American Invasion of Canada, 1775-1776* (New York, 1968)
Robert M. Hatch, *Thrust for Canada: The American Attempt on Quebec in 1775-1776* (Boston, 1979)

George F. G. Stanley, *Canada Invaded, 1775-1776* (Toronto, 1973)
Kenneth Roberts, *Arundel* (novel, 1944)

MAPS 8-9: NEW YORK

Bruce Bliven, Jr., *Battle for Manhattan* (New York, 1955)
Henry P. Johnston, *The Battle of Harlem Heights* (New York, 1897)

MAPS 10-11: TRENTON AND PRINCETON

Alfred Hoyt Bill, *The Campaign of Princeton, 1776-1777* (Princeton, 1948)
William M. Dwyer, *The Day is Ours! November 1776 - January 1777: An Inside View of the Battles of Trenton and Princeton* (New York, 1983)
William S. Stryker, *The Battles of Trenton and Princeton* (Boston and New York, 1898)

MAPS 12-18: THE SARATOGA CAMPAIGN

Harrison Bird, *March to Saratoga: General Burgoyne and the American Campaign, 1777* (New York, 1963)
Rupert Furneaux, *The Battle of Saratoga* (New York, 1971)

Hoffman Nickerson, *The Turning Point of the Revolution* (Boston and New York, 1928)
John S. Pancake, *1777: The Year of the Hangman* (University, Alabama, 1977)
Kenneth Roberts, *Rabble in Arms* (novel, 1933)

MAPS 19-22: THE PHILADELPHIA
CAMPAIGN

John F. Reed, *Campaign to Valley Forge, July 1, 1777 - December 19, 1777* (Philadelphia, 1965)
also Pancake, *op. cit.*

MAP 23

William S. Stryker, *The Battle of Monmouth* (Princeton, 1927)

MAPS 24-25: NEWPORT AND PENOBSCOT
BAY

John E. Cayford, *The Penobscot Expedition* (Orrington, Maine, 1976)
Paul F. Dearden, *The Rhode Island Campaign of 1778: Inauspicious Dawn of Alliance* (Providence, 1980)

MAP 26: STONY POINT AND PAULUS
HOOK

Henry P. Johnston, *The Storming of Stony Point* (New York, 1900)

MAP 27: WESTERN CAMPAIGNS

Dale Van Every, *A Company of Heroes: The American Frontier, 1775-1783* (New York, 1962)
A. H. Wright, *The Sullivan Expedition of 1779* (Ithaca, 1943)

MAP 28: SAVANNAH

Alexander A. Lawrence, *Storm over Savannah: The Story of Count d'Estaing and the Siege of the Town in 1779* (Athens, Ga., 1951)

MAP 29: THE WAR IN EUROPE

Gardner Allen, *A Naval History of the American Revolution*, 2 volumes (New York, 1940)
R. Ernest Duputy, Gay Hammerman, Grace P. Hayes, *The American Revolution, A Global War (New York, 1977)*

MAPS 30-33: THE SOUTHERN
CAMPAIGNS

John S. Pancake, *This Destructive War: The British Campaign in the Carolinas, 1780-1782* (University, Alabama, 1985)
M. F. Treacy, *Prelude to Yorktown: The Southern Campaign of Nathaniel Greene, 1780-1781* (Chapel Hill, 1962)

MAP 34: KING'S MOUNTAIN

Lyman C. Draper, *King's Mountain and Its Heroes* (Cincinnati, 1881)
Hank Messick, *King's Mountain: The Epic of the Blue Ridge "Mountain Men" in the American Revolution* (Boston, 1976)

MAPS 35-40: COWPENS TO EUTAW
SPRINGS

Burke Davis, *The Cowpens-Guilford Courthouse Campaign* Philadelphia, 1962)
Kenneth Roberts, *The Battle of Cowpens* (New York, 1958)
also Pancake and Treacy, *op. cit.*

MAPS 40-42: YORKTOWN

Burke Davis, *The Campaign That Won America: The Story of Yorktown* (Philadelphia, 1970)
Thomas J. Fleming, *Beat the Last Drum: The Siege of Yorktown, 1781* (New York, 1963)
Harold A. Larrabee, *Decision at the Chesapeake* (New York, 1964)